LONDON STREET FURNITURE

LONDON STREET FURNITURE

DAVID BRANDON & ALAN BROOKE

AMBERLEY

First published 2010

Amberley Publishing Plc
Cirencester Road, Chalford,
Stroud, Gloucestershire, GL6 8PE

www.amberleybooks.com

British Library Cataloguing in Publication Data.
A catalogue record for this book is available from the British Library.

ISBN 978 1 84868 294 8

Typeset in 10pt on 11pt Celeste Sans OT.
Typesetting by Amberley Publishing.
Printed in the UK.

CONTENTS

INTRODUCTION 7

ART DECO 10

BENCHES 14

BOLLARDS 16

BRIDGES 19

CABBIES' SHELTERS 24

CLOCKS 26

COAL-HOLE COVERS 28

COMMEMORATIVE PLAQUES 30

COMMEMORATIVE STATUES 37

DRINKING-FOUNTAINS 42

FIREMARKS 49

FOOTSCRAPERS 50

A POT-POURRI OF ASSORTED STREET FURNITURE – PART 1 52

GHOST ADVERTS 58

GHOST STREET SIGNS 62

HERALDRY 63

HOLBORN VIADUCT 66

HORSE-TROUGHS 67

LETTER-BOXES 69

LIGHTING 72

MILESTONES 76

MOUNTING BLOCKS 78

PLANE TREES	79
A POT-POURRI OF ASSORTED STREET FURNITURE – PART 2	80
POLICE BOXES	85
PORTERS' RESTS	86
PUBLIC CONVENIENCES	88
PUB SIGNS	92
PUMPS	98
RAILINGS	100
SHOP FRONTS AND SHOP SIGNS	102
STREET SIGNS	110
SUNDIALS	113
TELEPHONE BOXES	114
WELLS	119
A POT-POURRI OF ASSORTED STREET FURNITURE – PART 3	120

INTRODUCTION

This book intends to take a slightly whimsical look at the subject of street furniture in London. At the risk of offending the purist or the pedant, the authors primarily consider street furniture to be the fixtures and features found along or close to public roads, streets, and paths and such places as parks and public gardens. They must be visible in or from these places so we do not include items found inside buildings but may sometimes consider external architectural features, particularly if they are decorative. For the purposes of this work, we would contend that the objects concerned do not necessarily have to possess any particular utility value. For that reason, perhaps contentiously, we are happy to include such items as memorials and commemorative statues. Perhaps it is churlish to say that they have no utility value. They mean something to someone, or at least they presumably once did even if the person or event they commemorate is now largely forgotten.

Many of the items constituting street furniture had and many still do have the purpose of assisting those moving about London's streets, whether on foot, on horseback or in wheeled conveyances. A history of street furniture, which this is definitely not, would trace the evolution of much street furniture against the changing nature of London's traffic. In turn, pedestrians, horses, electric traction, and motor vehicles have all had different requirements and meeting these requirements has meant the development of items of street furniture appropriate to each transport medium.

It is of the nature of street furniture that much of it tends not to be noticed, even though many items are designed precisely for the purpose of being seen. Even large statues on plinths blocking the pavement or forming an obstacle around which traffic has to manoeuvre can easily be ignored. It is understandable that the Londoner on his or her daily movement around the capital does not bother with actually viewing such things but it is likely that many visitors do not really take much notice of them either. Some items of street furniture are actually advertisements of sorts. Pub signs are obvious examples and yet few people stop to analyse or admire the handiwork of the sign painter and this despite the fact that his work may be of the very highest order and that he has gone to great lengths to get the historical or other details right. Bollards are another example. They are there to try to prevent road-users hitting buildings, driving where vehicular traffic is forbidden or mounting the pavement. They are reminders to

Gothic Bollard, Commercial Street, E1.

the road-user but how many people actually ever give them more than a second glance. Perhaps it is their essentially mundane nature or 'everydayness' that means that many items of street furniture go largely ignored.

For all that, street furniture is part of the evidence of the past and the present of that living, ever-changing, and immensely complicated organism known as London. In this volume the authors do not attempt to list all the items which can be lumped together under the generic name of 'street furniture'. Rather, we consider samples, trying where possible to trace their history and to say where an example or two can be found with the proviso that time and tide do not necessarily wait for any bollard, shop sign, or redundant phone box in London. Street furniture is vulnerable to those we allow to plan and manage the streets supposedly on our behalf and to their counterparts, the unofficial vandals. These include yobs out on a binge, or motorists, whose crazed activities behind the wheel take a heavy toll on certain types of street furniture.

It will be obvious that we have a liking for the quirky and the off-beat, and we hope that our love and enthusiasm for London, and especially its peculiar and ill-considered features, comes across. We have gained great pleasure in poking about, teasing out much that is overlooked or forgotten, and we feel that we have learned a lot in doing so only to realise, at the same time, how much more there is to know about London and what its streets contain.

We largely restrict ourselves to what may loosely be called 'Central London' which is convenient for us because it means that we don't really have to define the area but we certainly do not stray into the fastnesses of outer suburban London. Also the emphasis tends towards the older items of street furniture. This may be because the authors are themselves in danger of becoming antiques. Actually, it's because older items are usually more interesting and we do not believe that people want to read about familiar, seemingly ubiquitous, items of street furniture, such as closed-circuit television cameras, for example. Again, we could not bring ourselves to look at street markings.

It is an undeniable fact of twenty-first century London life that the streets are in danger of disappearing under ever-growing amounts of street furniture. A very large number of these items are telling road users what they can't do in that particular location and their sheer proliferation means that increasingly they tend to confuse rather than to inform. It is dysfunctional and unattractive clutter. We do not like it and we feel that our readers, if any, are likely to share that view.

The choice of what has been included here is entirely that of the authors. We make no claim for the book being comprehensive or encyclopaedic. For example, readers will search in vain for an illustration, let alone the potted history, of the parking meter in London. This is not because we forgot them or even have a fierce antipathy towards the things. We just have not got round to including an example or two. They are unquestionably items of street furniture and they could appear in volume 2 if there ever is another volume. Even from our comparatively limited poking around in London, we have left many good items out. The problem is that in some of the areas of London, which throw up the richest crops of interesting or odd examples of street furniture, the seeker is only too aware that the best item of all may be lurking coyly around the next corner – the corner that you never go round because your attention is diverted by something else. It would not be unfair to say that the list of interesting items to be seen on London's streets is simply inexhaustible.

If acknowledgements are needed, we should thank ourselves for taking the photographs and Amberley Publishing for agreeing to publish this singular volume. If anything else deserves our gratitude, it is London itself for being such a wonderful place.

ART DECO

It may seem odd to have a section on Art Deco in a book about street furniture. However, we include it as part of our wide-ranging definition of the subject. That the style certainly features in London's street furniture cannot be denied.

Art Deco first made a significant impact at the 1925 *Exposition Internationale des Artes Decoratifs et Industriels*. There the contents of the British Pavilion made a very strong, if controversial, impression. Art Deco then took off and, with various concessions to national considerations, became an international style. The 1920s and 1930s were a difficult period for Britain. The end of the First World War confirmed the absolute world dominance of the USA. This meant that Britain had to get used to a very different economic and political role in the world from that which she had enjoyed for the best part of a century. Things that she still clung on to, and of which she was inordinately proud, included her empire, her maritime international trading links, and her pioneering role as an industrial nation. Art Deco was one way of celebrating these.

Many major commercial buildings built between the wars were faced with Portland stone which, when new and clean, was almost startlingly white. Such buildings did not stay pristine for long in London's then soot-laden air. Fortunately most of them have been cleaned in the last few decades. The BBC Broadcasting House in Portland Place, W1, was restored in 2005. Built in 1931, it has been likened to a battleship and certainly there is much that is aggressive about its 'prow' pointing towards Regent Street. Visually it bullies even other very large buildings in its vicinity. From the street furniture point of view, however, its hard lines are softened by Eric Gill's sculpture of Prospero and Ariel above the main door. There are also a number of sculpted reliefs by Gill on the building's façade including the charming 'Ariel piping to children' which is a reference to the BBC's late-lamented 'Children's Hour'.

A sculpture of monumental size can be seen on the façade of the former Imperial Airways Terminal Building at 157-197, Buckingham Palace Road. 'Speed Wings over the World' by E. R. Broadbent symbolises the task then being undertaken by the company, certainly something more glamorous (and probably more worthwhile) than that of the building's present occupants, the National Audit Office.

Surely one of London's most extraordinary modern buildings is the former Ideal House, National Radiator Company's Building, completed in 1929 at the junction of Great

Not Art Deco but Art Nouveau, Black Friar Pub, Queen Victoria Street, EC4. Both inside and out, this pub is a riot of whimsical Art Nouveau.

Marlborough Street and Argyle Street, SW1. This is now Palladium House. The architect was the American Raymond M. Hood, known for his flamboyant skyscrapers in New York. It is faced with shiny black granite which has earned it the nickname 'The Moor of Argyll Street', which can be taken in a number of ways. At street level most readily visible are the surrounds to the main entrance and the ground floor windows of what was a showroom for the Company. These are Persian-style enamel on bronze and they were designed by the Birmingham Guild of Handicraft. Is this Art Deco?

The heyday of the department store is without doubt over. Kensington High Street can still boast a few such emporia of which Barkers at Nos 63-97 has some treats for fans of a jazzy version of Art Deco. This building was completed in phases between 1927 and 1958. This has a number of bas-reliefs at upper levels. They show what, in 1938, were modern or even futuristic forms of transport, including a jet-engined passenger aircraft with a v-wing formation. There are also charming little carved vignettes of goods sold in the store, including cricket equipment and ladies' shoes, which seem to have dated remarkably little. The former Derry & Toms store of 1933, also in Kensington High Street, W8, has cast aluminium friezes, some of which depicts stylized crocodiles and other less readily-identified animals, and Portland stone bas-reliefs collectively known as 'Labour and Technology'.

11

The 'Spirit of Ecstasy', which adorns the top of the radiator on cars of the Rolls-Royce stable, is without a doubt a classic and universally recognised icon. The statue of Count Peter, which stands on top of the Art Deco stainless steel canopy of the Savoy Hotel in the Strand, WC1, is an icon too, easily seen by passers-by on the opposite side of the street. The Savoy Hotel dates from 1889, being built on the site of the Savoy Palace but it had become a little worn around the edges before a major refurbishment in 1926-9 which is when Count Peter took up his place.

The 1920s and 1930s were the great days of cinema in the United Kingdom and 'Gaumonts', 'Odeons', 'Plazas', 'Railtos', and others appeared like mushrooms on a warmish, damp autumn morning. These years were wracked by both structural and short-term economic changes including serious recession and economic decay in those parts of the country dependent on the staple industries which had been so successful during the Industrial Revolution. Although London and the south east were considerably less affected, there was a generalised sense of insecurity which the film industry was able to exploit. People wanted escapism which the fantasies of Hollywood supplied, and just for an hour or two they also wanted to be safe, warm, and comfortable and to forget the world outside. The most opulent picture palaces were like wombs and were designed to provide exactly that elusive secure ambience. The cinema industry based itself on larger-than-life fantasy and cinemas at the cutting edge were equally fantastic. Being built in the inter-war years, many of them incorporated Art Deco features as part of the glamorous image they wanted to create.

A barber's shop sign. Symbolically, this represents a bloodied bandage round an injured limb, recalling the work once performed by barber-surgeons. Such signs seem to be an endangered species. Fulham Palace Road, W6.

Here we give just two examples of these amazing buildings. The New Victoria Cinema of 1928-30, Wilton Road and Vauxhall Bridge Road, SW1, draws on a Germanic version of Art Deco. It has a Portland Stone frontage but sports the words 'Exit' and 'Stage Door' cast in stone and hiding ventilation grilles and a tiny easy-to-miss figure of Charlie Chaplin also masking a ventilation grille. There are bas-reliefs depicting different genres of cinema above the exit doors on the Wilton Road frontage. Second is the Odeon, 23-27, Leicester Square, WC2. This was designed to be the flagship of the developing Odeon brand and its tower can only be described as 'brash'. The cinema was built in 1937 and dominates the east side of the Square and, although renovated unsympathetically, it retains its striking Art Deco black polished granite frontage.

No. 55, Broadway, SW1, is an edifice like something out of an Orwellian phantasmagoria. It was built in 1927-9 as a headquarters for the ambitious group of companies which was intent on taking over the underground railways and the trams, bus, and later trolleybus services of Greater London. It is very much an inter-war building and displays some external sculpture of very considerable interest. They include two sculptures by Epstein dubbed respectively, 'Day' and 'Night'. The former was once described in the *Daily Express* newspaper as 'a prehistoric blood-sodden cannibal intoning a horrid ritual over a dead victim'. Other relief sculptures include examples by Eric Gill and Henry Moore. All have excited controversy over the years.

Finally, for anyone who is beginning to doubt whether there is any merit in this Art Deco, an external viewing of the Royal Institute of British Architects in Portland Place, W1, may have a restorative effect. Inside isn't bad either.

BENCHES

The Victorians were the first people to go in for providing seating available to all in such public places as streets and parks. While local authorities provided many benches and seats, others were often paid for privately as memorials for deceased relatives or friends and they frequently bore little plaques to that effect. Usually the framework was made of iron and the seat of wood. London has innumerable examples of benches erected over a period of almost two hundred years and they range in design from the simple, unadorned and totally functional to whimsical fantasies. Of the latter, some of the best are to be found on the Victoria Embankment. These include a set of benches in which the supports are in the form of camels, presumably to make Cleopatra's Needle, which is close by, feel at home. Just by way of variation, other benches have sphinxes to support them.

Camel Bench, Victoria Embankment, WC2.

Bicycles attached...

BOLLARDS

Bollards are familiar but widely abused pieces of street furniture. They have been in use at least since the eighteenth century when Dr Johnson is reputed always to have touched them for good luck when passing along the street. Doubtless, there are far more now than when he perambulated the streets of the city he came to love so dearly.

Bollards were originally put in place to prevent wheeled conveyances entering certain roadways or streets, especially narrow ones or dead-ends, for example. They also provided protection around the base of such items as statues and gateways but they now are particularly used to prevent vehicles mounting the pavement, either because of carelessness on the part of the driver, in an attempt to get round an obstacle in the road or, increasingly, for the purposes of parking. Few people study bollards with interest. Indeed, few people study street furniture with much interest. Their lives might be richer if they did. However, because bollards have the temerity to get in the way of motorists, most of who think they can do whatever they like in the streets as long as everyone else obeys the rules, they are frequently cursed by irate drivers. There's no point in taking it out on a bollard. It is, after all, only doing the job for which it was designed. In the 1990s, a new purpose was found for bollards – to thwart the designs of ram-raiders. Bollards for this purpose are usually short and stout. Concrete bollards are inferior. They have little of the durability of their iron brethren. Bell bollards are a comparatively recent innovation and are particularly useful for deflecting the tyres of large moving vehicles.

Most bollards to be seen today date from after 1815. At that time, the muzzles of the cannon on many captured ships were appropriated and, with the open end filled with a small iron dome, they were ideal for use as bollards. They appeared in large numbers on London's streets and some can still be seen, although later bollards were sometimes cast in imitation of redundant ships' cannon, complete with the iron dome. Occasionally, bollards had one or more rings built into them which meant that they doubled as tethering posts. At the junction of Gracechurch Street and Eastcheap, EC3, stands a formidable black and white bollard. It is also dual-purpose, acting as a bollard and a ventilator for the adjacent underground toilets.

Acorn-topped bollard, Balcombe
Street, NW1.

Kensington and Chelsea Borough bollard,
Observatory Gardens, W8.

Rather superior bollard, St Paul's
Churchyard, EC4.

City of London bollard.

Emaciated bollard, Carter Lane, EC4.

Bollards galore, Shoe Lane, EC4.

BRIDGES

Road and pedestrian bridges are streets, even if not of the normally recognised kind. They certainly have fittings which can be described as furniture.

Battersea Bridge is the westernmost bridge and in the area of London we are considering. The first bridge was of timber and was put up in 1771-2. Perhaps surprisingly, it was the first bridge in London to have lighting installed. This was oil in 1799, replaced by gas in 1824. It was not a particularly robust bridge and it did not help that vessels on the river frequently hit it. As traffic across it built up, it was generally agreed that a new bridge was needed and this was built by Sir Joseph Bazalgette and opened in 1890.

Locals had been fond of the old bridge and so had artists who liked to portray it as a rather rustic and romantic object. Its most famous depiction was by James Whistler (1834-1903) in *Nocturne: Blue and Gold.* This was in an Impressionist style somewhat reminiscent of Monet, and caused controversy which turned to laughter when a learned judge publicly asked Whistler, 'Which part of the picture is the bridge?'

The new bridge was of cast iron. The parapet consists of a series of fine arabesque arches while the main spans display ornamental shields and decorative foliage in the spandrels.

Albert Bridge joins Chelsea and the Battersea Park area south of the river. Most people agree that it is a quaint bridge. It was opened in 1873 and is of unusual design, the roadway being supported both by cable-stays and suspension chains. Structural problems have plagued the bridge almost from the start and it does not really have the robustness needed for the purposes of handling heavy modern road traffic. In the 1950s, it was intended to knock it down and replace it with a masonry bridge. The Albert Bridge may not be much good as a bridge but it clearly generated much affection and storms of protest ensured that it remained where it was. It is now a listed building and has been repainted in attractive (?) colours but it is at night when it comes into its own. It is festooned with lights like a linear Christmas tree.

The most interesting and unusual item of street furniture that the Albert Bridge can boast is a notice at each end erected by The Royal Borough of Kensington and Chelsea which reads: 'All troops to break step at the approach to Albert Bridge'. It is thought that their synchronised steps could set up vibrations and cause undue stress to the structure.

Chelsea Bridge is the third of the road crossings joining Chelsea and Battersea. It was opened in 1858 by Queen Victoria and was known at first as the 'Victoria Bridge', a name which did not last. It was a suspension bridge employing cast and wrought iron. The bridge proved inadequate for coping with ever-increasing amounts of road traffic and it was replaced in 1937 by a new suspension bridge. Its design was deliberately kept fairly simple but it is well-known for the odd-looking lamp-posts topped with, of all things, golden galleons and, more understandably, with the fine heraldic insignia of the LCC and the boroughs of Battersea and Kensington and Chelsea. Like its near neighbour, the Albert Bridge, Chelsea Bridge is decorated with a mass of lights during the hours of darkness.

Vauxhall Bridge was opened in 1816 and was the first cast-iron bridge over the Thames in London. At first it was called 'Regent's Bridge' but this name never really caught on. In 1906, a replacement bridge was opened under the auspices of the LCC. It consisted of steel arches on granite piers. Facing outwards from the piers are large sculptures which represent Local Government, Education, Science, Agriculture, Architecture, Engineering, Pottery, and Fine Arts. We hesitate to call these 'street furniture' because they can really only be seen from the river or the bank nearby, but we excuse ourselves on the grounds that they are part of the structure of the bridge which is, after all, a street. The sculpture called 'Architecture', for example, is a scale model of St Paul's Cathedral. A good view of this can be had by climbing up onto the parapet on the west side of the bridge and jumping off, preferably with a parachute.

Spanning the river between Westminster and Lambeth was a bridge which opened in 1862. This was the first Lambeth Bridge close to where the former horse ferry had been. It was a suspension bridge and was not very successful because of a number of structural and design faults which meant that in 1910 it had to be closed to vehicular traffic. A replacement bridge of steel was opened in July 1932. It is a fairly workaday bridge which does the job required of it. Its most notable ornamentations which can, thankfully, be seen by pedestrians without leaning over the parapet endangering their lives, are the well-known obelisks placed at the approaches to either end of the bridge. They are topped by what most people think are motifs representing pineapples. The reasons why pineapples were chosen have always been the subject of speculation.

The original Westminster Bridge was a stone structure opened in 1750 which was only the second bridge to be built across the Thames where it flowed through the Metropolis. By 1750, a relief for London Bridge had been desperately needed. It was concerning the view from this masonry bridge that Wordsworth, in 1802, wrote his well-known sonnet 'Composed upon Westminster Bridge'. The first Westminster Bridge may have been a fine place for poets to stand and compose verses about the enthralling beauty of the sleeping city, but almost as soon as it had been built, concerns were expressed about its structural stability. The official 'umming and arring' was even more obfuscating and protracted than normal but a decision was eventually reached that a new bridge would have to be built. This was opened in 1862 and was of iron with granite piers. At the southern end of the bridge stands a rather splendid, muscular-looking lion made of the artificial Coade stone. Painted red, this beast once stood sentinel over the entrance to the appropriately-named Red Lion Brewery on the South Bank. This lion had something of a peripatetic existence after the brewery closed but it was placed on its current pedestal in 1966. For lovers of the erotic, the northern end of the bridge sports a sculpture in bronze of Queen Boudicca (we still think of her as Boadicea) with her two daughters who, perfectly understandably in view of the fact that they appear to be going into battle, are bare-breasted. Clearly, Boudicca was a dominatrix and she is shown at the reins of her war chariot complete with its scythes. Small boys gazing at the sculpture are faced with an appalling dilemma. Which is more fascinating, the breasts or the scythes?

Somewhat overshadowed by this display of rampant femininity, but close by on the steps from the Embankment to Westminster Bridge, is a curious and rather forlorn-looking green kiosk. It contains gauges used for measuring the tides in the Thames.

The first Waterloo Bridge was a celebrity among bridges. It was designed by John Rennie and it was opened in 1817 on the second anniversary of the Battle of Waterloo. It drew admirers from near and afar and it looked a solid as the Rock of Gibraltar. Structural problems were evident as early as 1833, but in 1923 settlement of the piers meant that a temporary iron bridge had to be built alongside. The bridge was suffering from scouring of its foundations and was not standing up well to increasing amounts of heavier road traffic. Londoners were very attached to the bridge, as were aesthetes and others, but controversially the decision was taken to demolish it in 1936 and replace it with a reinforced concrete bridge, which opened in 1942. It was designed by Sir Giles Gilbert Scott who did rather well out of the Thames because he also designed the Bankside and Battersea Power Stations which depended on the river for their coal supplies. Even the previously querulous aesthetes were quite pleased with its appearance, especially since it was faced with Portland Stone. Fans of street furniture will find little to drool over on Waterloo Bridge but it would have seemed churlish not to have mentioned it.

Blackfriars Bridge between the City and Southwark was opened in 1769, being the third bridge to span the Thames in London. By the early 1830s, it was experiencing problems, not least scouring of the piers which had been considerably exacerbated when Old London Bridge was removed and the flow of the Thames speeded up as a result. A replacement bridge was opened in 1869 by Queen Victoria on the same day that she declared Holborn Viaduct operational. This bridge was of wrought and cast iron on granite piers and was widened in 1910. At street level the granite piers are topped by rather curious recesses which have been likened to pulpits and are said to have been designed in this fashion as reminders of the erstwhile Blackfriars Monastery which was nearby. Visible from the bridge, and not street furniture but inevitably drawing the eye of pedestrians, are the gaunt remains of the first Blackfriars railway bridge. This was built in 1864 by the London, Chatham, and Dover Railway but became surplus to requirements and was demolished in 1985. The massive cast-iron piers are still in place topped by the extravert, colourful insignia of the LCDR.

The Millennium Bridge is superb to look at and to look from but has little to offer the aficionado of street furniture.

Southwark Bridge was opened in 1819 as a three-arch cast-iron bridge linking the Mansion House area of the City with Southwark. This bridge never caught the imagination despite having a central span of no less than 73 metres, the largest-ever in cast iron. It had a steep gradient which could make it difficult for horse-drawn traffic and its approaches were awkward. A steel bridge with five arches replaced it in 1921. Somehow it has still not caught on and seems underused even given the revival of the Southwark side of the river at this point. Under the approach arches of the bridge, on both sides of the river, there are slate murals. Those on the south show scenes of the old Frost Fairs on the Thames, those on the north depict the previous Southwark Bridge.

Contemporary illustrations and artists' impressions show that Old London Bridge was most definitely a street, lined at one time with buildings almost along its entire length when it must have had more furniture than you could shake a stick at. The Romans built the first bridge, a timber structure. This and various wooden replacements underwent chequered lives until the building of the first masonry bridge began around 1176. Records show that it had houses on it by 1201. This bridge was at the centre of London's history for centuries. One item of street furniture which the bridge boasted in medieval times but which, thankfully, can no longer be seen, were the heads of executed traitors placed conspicuously on tall spikes on the gateways as a silent but salutary lesson to all of the wages of sin. The houses were removed in the middle of the eighteenth century, by which time not only was a replacement for London Bridge needed, but also additional bridges across the Thames were urgently required. A new bridge designed by Sir John Rennie was opened in 1831 and this did a fine job until the 1960s, when it was decided that a new bridge was needed. The present pre-stressed concrete cantilevered bridge was its replacement and can best be described as 'functional'. As is well-known, the earlier bridge was carefully dismantled and re-erected in Arizona for an oil-rich American tycoon with more money than sense. The story that this transatlantic plutocrat thought he was buying Tower Bridge is apocryphal. The Americans did not get the entire bridge. On the south side, one arch of Rennie's bridge can still be found along with a set of stairs known as 'Nancy's Steps'. These stairs feature in *Oliver Twist* by Dickens and a plaque reveals all. Three stones also from Rennie's bridge can be seen in the churchyard of St Magnus the Martyr, Lower Thames Street, EC3. A stone alcove containing a seat can be seen in Victorian Park, E9, and another in the courtyard of Guy's Hospital. It is the only remaining seat from the old London Bridge.

If anyone asked the authors which bridge in London was their favourite, they would have no hesitation in stating that it was Tower Bridge. The word 'iconic' has become grossly overused and abused but it can certainly be applied in this particular case. For nigh on a century, this was the only bridge across the Thames below London Bridge. Better road communication between the docks and wharves on each side of the Thames that lined the Pool of London had become increasingly urgent in the nineteenth century given the huge increase in maritime trade through London. Additionally, large enclaves of working-class housing had spread east from London Bridge on both sides of the Thames, the wage-earners of the families largely being employed in the docks or in associated industries. The need to move goods and people from one side of the river to the other put huge strains on London Bridge. A new bridge was required downstream from London Bridge but, situated as it would be in the Pool of London, it would need to be designed to allow ships with tall masts to pass by unhindered. This was a daunting prospect given the low banks on either side of the Thames. Typically of Victorian times, the design of the bridge was the subject of a competition and it was won by John Wolfe-Barry who came up with the idea of a bascule bridge with a lifting roadway. It was opened in 1894. His brief required the bridge to harmonise with the Norman architecture of the Tower, close by the northern end of the bridge. This it certainly does not do because the towers of the bridge are in a riotously eclectic neo-Gothic bearing little resemblance to any designated architectural style and most certainly not Norman. However, underneath the skin as it were, was the very latest Victorian technology – hydraulic machinery powered by steam for raising the bascules. In 1976, electric power replaced steam. On the western approach to the north end of the bridge stands a curious blue cast iron column with no apparent purpose. It is actually a chimney which served the fireplace in a room below, occupied by men who worked on the bridge.

CABBIES' SHELTERS

We all have an image in our minds of the horse of a Hansom cab clopping its way across the cobbles and granite setts of Victorian London. These beguilingly simple vehicles were a ubiquitous feature of London's streets in the second half of the nineteenth century before they were forced to retreat, albeit quite slowly at first, before the advance of the internal combustion taxi cab. This advance eventually became inexorable. The Hansom cab was designed by Joseph Aloysius Hansom (1803-82). He was born in York and his day job was being an architect.

Cabbies worked long hours in all kinds of weather and sometimes they were so busy that there was no gap between fares. On other occasions they had to wait around for business or they wanted some refreshment and some good crack with their mates. To provide them with necessary facilities, shelters were put up in various parts of Central London. The first to appear were in 1875. There were at least 100 of these but only a handful of them remain. They provided a necessary and much-appreciated service for a perhaps surprisingly large body of men. There were about 11,000 Hansom cabs and other horse-drawn conveyances plying for hire in London in 1896 and over 20,000 cabbies.

These shelters were made of timber, painted a rather inconspicuous green and almost rustic in appearance. They had steeply pitched roofs and normally a small chimney which allowed the smoke from the stove to escape. A fine working example of these shelters can be found behind Temple Tube Station. When we say working, we mean that it provides refreshments but no longer necessarily for cabbies.

Above: Taxi Man's Shelter, Temple Place, WC2. A survivor, although no longer quite used for its original purpose.

Right: Cigarette stubber. These unattractive receptacles are now found in their hundreds of thousands around the Metropolis. New items of street furniture keep appearing. Now there are little bins into which people can drop their chewing gum rather than letting it fall to the pavement where it forms a disgusting semi-permanent patina. Somebody once said, 'A human chewing gum and a cow chewing the cud. The cow looked more intelligent.'

CLOCKS

London has a plethora of clocks in public places. Even the interesting ones are almost too numerous to mention. However, here are a few worth looking at. The clock of St Dunstan-in-the-West, Fleet Street, EC4, was made in 1671 and shows Gog and Magog who berate the bell with their staves every quarter of an hour. Liberty's, that extraordinary mock-timber emporium that would look more at home in Chester than it does in Regent Street, has a little scenario every quarter of an hour in which St George can be seen vainly pursuing a dragon. At Fortnum & Mason, Piccadilly, W1, every hour miniatures of the two named gentlemen emerge from the wall and bow to each other while a carillon sounds. In the City at St Mary at Hill, EC3, a very fine clock protrudes from the wall, typical of many similar public timepieces. A fine Art Deco clock adorns the frontage of the former headquarters of the *Daily Telegraph* at No.120, Fleet Street, EC4. Less spectacular but no less worthy Art Deco clocks can be seen at BBC Broadcasting House, Portland Place, W1, and a particularly attractive one at Alkit's clothing store, Cambridge Circus, W2.

St Mary Abbots, Kensington High Street, has a clock which sounds the quarters but for whatever reason, when the tower was built, they omitted to fit a dial and so it is the clock which is heard but never seen.

Above: Clock in Pied Bull Yard, WC1.

Right: Clock Boswell House, off Boswell Street, WC1.

COAL-HOLE COVERS

Coal-hole covers are what might be described as 'underfoot' street furniture. London once could show off tens of thousands of these interesting objects because they were built into the pavement at the front of houses that had cellars under the road. The holes were just the right size to allow deliveries of coal to be made straight from the sack by gravity through the hole and after the cover had of course been temporarily removed. This saved the possible dirt and disruption that could occur when coal was carried through the house to wherever it was to be stored. They were nearly always found serving the houses of the well-to-do, especially in the three or four storey houses which were built in vast numbers in certain districts of London, roughly in the period from 1750 to 1900. Occasionally the houses they fronted have gone and we are left with the anomaly of coal-hole covers outside more modern buildings which were never designed for heating with solid fuel.

These covers were made of cast-iron and huge numbers have disappeared during street 'improvements' and for various other reasons simply because, until comparatively recently, they were thought of as virtually worthless. Most of them date from the mid-nineteenth century to around 1900 and were designed to be flush with the pavement although they usually had a slightly raised pattern to prevent pedestrians slipping on them when it was wet. Many of them are about twelve inches in diameter – any larger and it was thought that burglars would use them to gain entry to the premises. Small they may be but many are real objets d'art in decorative ironwork. They come in a wide range of designs including chevrons, stars, trefoils, and quatrefoils, and most of them include the name of the iron-founder who manufactured them. Some simply bear the name of the manufacturer. In fact, the names are interesting because many covers were made in London and are a reminder of the frequently-forgotten fact that London was at one time a major industrial centre. An example is Hayward Brothers who had a foundry in Union Street, Southwark, SE1.

Coal-hole covers might have continued their unobtrusive and obscure existence had it not been for the growth in interest in Victoriana in the 1960s. An exhibition of actual coal-hole covers and rubbings of lost examples was held in London in 1962 and, far from being the hopeless non-event its detractors gleefully predicted, it attracted considerable interest. John (later Sir John) Betjeman, who opened the

A collection of coal-hole covers around Bloomsbury.

proceedings, gave an impassioned speech about the aesthetic and historical value of coal-hole covers and how they needed to be preserved before they disappeared for ever from London's streets. Parts of Kensington, Pimlico, Bloomsbury, and Paddington are happy hunting grounds for those seeking to record these small iron objects. People who make a hobby out of doing so are referred to, among other things, as 'operculists', a word derived from the Latin for cover or lid.

There are many other covers relevant to the various services scattered around London's streets. Fire hydrant indicators are very common but the authors felt that this was too specialised a subject to be worthy of more than a passing mention. Perhaps we got that wrong.

COMMEMORATIVE PLAQUES

London is a place which oozes history and history is made by people. Accidents of birth and other forms of happenstance can propel rogues, incompetents, and total nonentities into prominent positions during their lifetimes and then into the history books. The names of people of merit with genuinely great achievements to their names may deservedly live on after their deaths. This kind of fame is capricious, however, because the past is full of unsung heroes who have benefited humanity in large or small ways but have neither sought nor received acclamation while others who have done very little to boast about have nevertheless succeeded in their burning desire to achieve celebrity.

So it is that the commemorative plaques of London are a somewhat arbitrary if fascinating feature of London's streets. These plaques first made their appearance from 1867, being sponsored by the Royal Society of Arts. Plaques disappear – sometimes they are stolen, sometimes the person they celebrate goes out of favour, or the plaque itself falls into disrepair, is removed, and not replaced. The building on which the plaque is displayed may be demolished and for any number of reasons no replacement is undertaken. The earliest surviving RSA plaques date from 1875 and one of them recalls the memory of Napoleon III (1808-73) who resided at No. 1c, King Street, St James's, SW1, in 1848. He was a political opportunist of the first order and it was his stupidity that led to the Franco-Prussian War of 1870 and a catastrophic defeat for France. In 1901, the London County Council took over responsibility for selecting the people to be commemorated and erecting the plaques. By the time the GLC assumed the responsibility in 1965, almost 400 plaques had been put up. The GLC was wound up in 1985 whereupon English Heritage took on and considerably accelerated the process of installing plaques. Now there is something approaching 1000 official blue plaques in Greater London. But then we now live in the age of celebrities.

There are a large and ever-growing number of other plaques erected since the 1900s by local authorities, various associations and organisations, and even private individuals. The rectangular blue glazed plaques erected by the Corporation are familiar sights in the City of London. Equally familiar are the green plaques put in place by the City of Westminster. Other local authorities who have erected plaques in what might reasonably be described as 'Central London' include the Borough Councils of Camden, Islington, Tower Hamlets, Southwark, Kensington and Chelsea, and Hackney. Among the extremely

Commit no nuisance, The Borough, SE1.

AA Plaque, Fleet Street, EC4. By no means all plaques are blue plaques!

diverse range of other organisations who have sponsored plaques are: Colonial Dames of America; The Association of Anaesthetists of Great Britain and Ireland; the National Art Collections Fund; the Royal Television Society; the Anglo-Brazilian Society; the Royal Navy; Comic Heritage; the Commonwealth of Australia and the Cromwell Association.

It is only to be expected that London's plaques would provide a reflection on the rich diversity that is the history of the Metropolis. A few oddities among these plaques follow:

Displayed on Red Lion Antiques Arcade, Portobello Road, W11, a very controversial plaque reads, 'On this site Susan Garth launched London's first antiques market, making the Portobello Road an international institution.' The plaque was put up in 1975, despite considerable opposition based on the fact that there were antique stalls trading in the area before she set up business and that she was still alive at the time; it was felt that the award of a plaque should be posthumous.

8, Wilton Street, SW1. The plaque at this address celebrates the life and works of Thomas Gray (1827-61), author of his immortal *Anatomy* which, since its appearance in 1853, has provided a standard work of reference for medical students. The plaque was put in place by the LCC but for some reason is basically brown as opposed to the usual LCC blue.

98, Curtain Road, EC2, displays a Borough of Hackney plaque announcing that Holywell Priory formerly existed on this site where there was also a sacred spring. The monastic establishment was founded in the 1150s and dissolved in the late 1530s, but the former presence of pure, pellucid waters gushing to the surface given the current nature of the district seems highly incongruous.

27, Edwardes Square, W8, displays a plaque put up by the Dead Comics Society to the memory of the camp comedian Frankie Howerd. He lived from 1922 to 1997 but the plaque wrongly gives his date of birth as 1917.

At 69-76, Long Acre, WC2, is a Westminster Council plaque to the little-known Denis Johnson (c. 1760-1833) who in 1819 unveiled the 'Hobby-Horse'. This was the primitive ancestor of the modern bicycle. The rider sat on the saddle and propelled the device using his legs. The machine was made of wood and iron and was considerably lighter than similar devices around at the time. However, it incurred considerable ridicule despite the fact that on the flat the rider could achieve a speed of up to 10mph. The rims of the wheels were solid and rattling on this contraption along cobbled streets and, over granite setts, must have brought tears to the eyes of its user.

Laystall Street, EC1, close to Clerkenwell, is in the district once known as 'Little Italy' by virtue of the large number of Italian ex-pats who lived there and gave it a distinctive character. No. 10 has a plaque of unusual design dedicated to the memory of Giuseppe Mazzini (1805-72), the Italian nationalist leader. A similar plaque can be found close by at No. 5, Hatton Garden. Both were erected privately.

Deep in the heart of the City stands No. 27, Clement's Lane, EC4. A privately-sponsored plaque tells anyone who reads it that in 1784 Dositey Obradovich lived on the site. In case this does not provide much enlightenment, it adds that he was an eminent Serbian man of letters and his country's first Minister of Education.

Set in the pavement on a traffic island at the junction of the Edgware and Bayswater Roads in W2 is a circular plaque declaring that it is the site of 'Tyburn Tree', the notorious

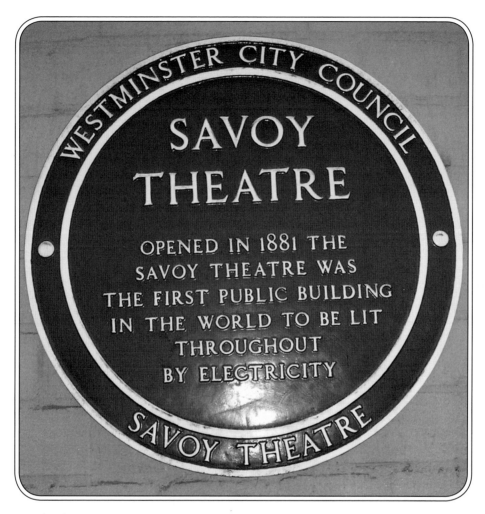

Blue Plaque, Carting Lane, WC2.

site at which tens of thousands of public executions were carried out from around the late twelfth century until the year 1783.

Perhaps a little out of 'Central London' and definitely off the most well-trodden tourist trails is a plaque erected by the Stepney Historical Trust at Noble Court, Cable Street, E1. It commemorates an eminent local boxer, Jack (Kid) Berg, born nearby in 1909. He reached the peak of his career around 1930. The plaque gives his nickname as the 'Whitechapel Windmill' when in fact he was known as the 'Whitechapel Whirlwind'. Cable Street gained fame in 1936 when it was blocked by local residents led by members of the Communist Party of Great Britain. They turned out in huge numbers successfully to prevent the passage of a march by Sir Oswald Mosley's British Union of Fascists which had been designed as a provocation to the large numbers of Jews who lived in this part of the East End.

Blue plaque to Elizabeth Garrett Anderson, Upper Berkeley Street, W1.

Blue Plaque, Hatton Garden, EC1. Not everyone would agree that Maxim contributed much to the lot of mankind.

Blue Plaque, Grove Road, E3.

Plaque, Historic Southwark. 103, Borough High Street.

City of London Plaque, Fleet Street, EC4.

Fleet Street, EC4. Fleet Street and its environs provide a rich crop of plaques and indeed of other kinds of street furniture.

COMMEMORATIVE STATUES

Here we take a look at some of London's open-air free-standing commemorative statues. Such statues can be said to be the product of the European Renaissance and they first appeared in this country in the seventeenth century. It is no coincidence that at least ten of London's statues are depicted in the clothes of ancient Greece and Rome. It seems incongruous or even slightly ridiculous for the statue of a nineteenth century British politician such as William Huskisson to show its subject draped in a toga. However, it was perhaps not entirely inappropriate given that almost all those who then rose to the top of the political hierarchy had received classical educations and looked to Greece and Rome as the fountainheads of inspiration for oratory and political theory.

Seemingly the first to be erected in London was at the top of Whitehall in 1676 and it commemorated Charles I. It is not surprising that after Sir Robert Peel, who represented the industrial bourgeoisie rather than Britain's traditional land-owning class, became Prime Minister, politicians and others were usually depicted in contemporary dress.

The French Revolution had a seismic impact in Britain – ideas of liberty, equality and fraternity absolutely terrified the British ruling class. These concepts were in due course replaced by the aggressive imperialism of Bonaparte who very nearly took over the entire world. At one time Britain was virtually the only nation that defied his might. Britain needed her heroes to emphasise the continuity of her military, cultural, and political life, even if only to contrast it with the volatility of the ways in which the French and the upstart Bonaparte did things. The age of the statue of the country's fighting heroes began, although it was some time before many of them appeared on the streets of London.

The idea of commemoration is not just one of memory – it may also be about making statements and statuary unquestionably reflects the minds and mores of the rich and powerful in society and to a lesser extent that of the populace as a whole. Statues caught on. From 1676 until the 1820s, those erected in the open air in London averaged one a decade. From the 1830s through to the 1850s, five were erected per decade and then from the 1860s to the 1920s, the average was eleven or twelve. Much of this time consisted of the years of Britain's seemingly almost unassailable world dominance and the confidence and smug sense of self-righteousness that went with it. The Victorians and Edwardians were great hero-worshippers. Admittedly, some of those commemorated in statues during that period, in reality, had feet of clay. Since that time this kind of adulation has largely tailed off. Those currently glorified are more likely to be pop music or film stars, leading footballers, and media 'celebrities'. In most cases, the fame they have is likely to prove transient at best and few, if any, will be remembered in statuary. New statues do continue to be unveiled but there is a tendency for them to be less a glorification of the so-called 'great' figures of Britain's past and more a reflection of the more diverse society that comes with globalism. They are also a reflection of Britain's relative decline in world terms and her consequent confused identity and marked lack of belief in herself and her appropriate role in the twenty-first century.

The funding for almost all of London's statues has come from public subscriptions of admirers and well-wishers and not as the result of any government attempt to foster patriotism or loyalty through the medium of outdoor statues of the great and the good. Many bureaucratic hoops have always had to be jumped through but it is likely that the pressures caused by these have built up greatly in the last few decades. It is likely that Londoners have always derived more pleasure from mocking new statues than applauding them. That, overall, is probably a healthy response. Like so many items of street furniture, it is probable that the majority of commemorative statues exist seen but largely unnoticed and that very few people stop to read the inscriptions or to ponder on the achievements so fulsomely described on the plinths.

Here we will consider a number of London's outdoor statues and where better to start than with the earliest of all, that of Charles I. This was completed in 1633 and embellished a private estate in Surrey until 1676 when it was transported to the top of Whitehall and re-erected where it has stood ever since. Charles was a self-important, arrogant little man of poor judgement which might have mattered little had he not been propelled into the unexpected role of King because of the premature death of his elder brother. He gained a reputation for being untrustworthy because he frequently made promises which he did not keep nor had he ever had any intention of keeping. He found himself on a collision course with Parliament which he regarded as little more than a milch cow to provide him with funds and a rubber stamp for his diktats. His theory of absolutism and the divine right of kings was an anachronism in a country developing the economic and ideological framework needed for its transition into becoming the first major industrial nation. Facing defeat in the Civil War, he entered into secret negotiations with foreign countries to come to his aid and this led him to be arraigned for treason. He was executed in Whitehall on 30 January 1649. He went to his death with great courage and dignity.

The history of the statue is interesting. It is the work of a French monarchist sculptor called Hubert Le Sueur who was an expert in casting in bronze and the statue was ordered by Lord Weston, the Lord High Commissioner, who put it up on his estate. In 1650, it was sequestered on the orders of Parliament and sold for scrap. The man who bought it was a cutler and claimed that it was melted down to provide him with raw material for his trade. In fact, it was hidden away and brought out again with the Restoration. Le Sueur had been instructed to portray Charles as a six-footer astride his horse rather than the less than five-footer he actually was. The statue was situated close to where the King had been executed and on the spot where there had been an Eleanor Cross. This had fallen out of favour during the Commonwealth and most of it had been taken away for building stone. The statue was given a corrugated iron shelter in the First World War because of aerial bombing by Zeppelins and in the Second World War it was first put in a similar shelter and then removed for safe keeping. Those who think that Charles was a martyr and that the Stuarts should be restored to the throne lay wreaths at the base of the statue on the anniversary of his execution.

Compared to his second son who became James II, Charles I was a positive wiseacre. A grandiloquent bronze statue of James II stands outside the National Gallery. He is shown in the garb of a Roman hero. James indeed in real life had a fine bearing and upright carriage but these only flattered to deceive. He had no sense of humour but is thought to have obtained great pleasure from watching the infliction of torture. There have been many stupid English monarchs but few took stupidity and pig-headedness to the heights achieved by James. He succeeded his elder brother Charles to the throne in 1685 and from then it was downhill all the way. He had all the stubbornness and lack of perception of his father but he fatally tried to combine a return to absolutism with the fanaticism of a convert to Catholicism who seemed bent on bringing England back into the Catholic fold. His short reign ended in December 1688 after the virtually unopposed invasion of William of Orange. He fled into exile but not before taking the precaution of dropping the Great Seal into the Thames. His swift departure led to it being decreed that he had abdicated. Everyone except the English Catholics called for three cheers.

It was only to be expected that the statue of this inept man had something of a chequered career. Erected late in 1685, it was first located in the gardens behind Whitehall. In 1897, it was relocated to the garden of Gwdyr House in Whitehall but its stay there was brief and in 1902, it was taken down and stored in a box in the garden. Whether or not the statue should be put on display again became a matter for bitter public debate but in due course it found itself in St James's Park near the Admiralty. On the outbreak of the Second World War it was taken down once again and stored for safe keeping in Aldwych tube station. After the war, the statue again became a matter of controversy and it ended up outside the National Gallery. Is this its last resting place?

Behind St Clement Dane's Church, Strand, stands a 6 ft tall statue of Dr Samuel Johnson (1709-84). It was sculpted by Percy Fitzgerald, paid for by him and unveiled by him. He was an avid admirer of Johnson. Although he was a native of Lichfield in Staffordshire, Johnson somehow is the archetype of the man who moved to London and there found his happy niche. His feelings for his adopted home are summed in his famous statement, 'No, sir, when a man is tired of London, he is tired of life, for there is in London all that life can afford.' Called by Tobias Smollett, 'The Great Cham of Literature' ('cham' meaning 'king'), he became the leading figure in London's literary circles.

Johnson was a large, somewhat awkward-looking, and dishevelled man. One of his contemporaries said that he 'dressed like a scarecrow and ate like a cormorant'. Another observer, more spitefully, said, 'His manners were sordid, supercilious and brutal'. He was gregarious, witty, generous to friends, a great raconteur, and reckoned to be good company. He suffered, however, from hypochondria and melancholia. On those rare occasions when he walked through London's streets alone, he waved his arms about and was clearly engaged in an intense emotional conversation with himself. He liked

Statue of William Hogarth (1697-1764), Chiswick High Road, W4.

Dr Johnson's cat, Hodge. Gough Square, EC4.

to remind people of his provincial roots by over-emphasising his Staffordshire accent. Although enjoying many sports when he was young, as he got older his afflictions mounted up. He had asthma, gout, dropsy, rheumatoid arthritis, smallpox and bronchitis, and suffered a stroke about a year before he died. With all this lot, it is all the more surprising that he kept a sharp sense of humour throughout. He died of emphysema, kidney disease and dropsy.

Probably Johnson's greatest achievement was his acclaimed *Dictionary of the English Language.* Johnson greatly enjoyed the company of women and married a widow twenty years his senior who predeceased him. He had various affairs but his greatest passion was probably for Mrs Thrale, the wife of a wealthy brewer. His affair with her ended abruptly, and to his great distress, when her husband died and she married an Italian. He was scornful of women preachers, remarking, 'A woman's preaching is like a dog's walking on its hind legs. It is not done well, but you are surprised to find it done at all.' He had a passionate dislike of Americans and said, 'I am willing to love all mankind, except an American.' He liked children and loved animals, having a cat called Hodge who he fed with copious quantities of oysters.

Another great Londoner was John Wilkes (1727-97). He is presented in bronze and makes a formidable figure, 8 ft 6 in tall, and stands on a 4 ft pedestal at the junction of Fetter Lane and New Fetter Lane in the City. The statue was unveiled in 1988. Wilkes was a radical politician, agitator, democrat, demagogue, and rake.

It is likely that having something wrong with you is a necessary if not a sufficient condition of becoming an MP. Perhaps those kids who were mocked in the school playground or humiliated by callous teachers in the classroom decide to get their own back by becoming MPs and tormenting everyone without prejudice. Wilkes belonged to the so-called 'Hellfire Club' of high-born roués which conducted its depraved activities on the Dashwood Estate at West Wycombe in Buckinghamshire. Wilkes and his fellow-members delighted in crude, vulgar, and offensive behaviour. The son of a wealthy distiller, Wilkes should have furthered his financial prospects when he married a rich heiress but he quickly worked his way through both his expectations and hers. As so many others of his generation, he bribed the electors and became an MP because MPs could not be arrested for debt. He then became a gadfly in Parliament, hurling scathing and inventive insults particularly at the Tory leaders. He started a newspaper, the *North Briton*, which sent shivers up the spines of the political elite because it campaigned ferociously against corruption in high places and for political reforms, including a widening of the franchise.

Wilkes was known for his thoroughgoing contempt for George III. At a large dinner party in Paris attended by the Prince of Wales, Wilkes got up and to universal amazement proposed a toast to the health of the English King. The puzzled Prince afterwards took Wilkes on one side and asked him how long he had harboured solicitous thoughts about his father. 'Only since I had the pleasure of your Royal Highness's acquaintance,' was Wilkes' instant response. Apparently the Prince thought that Wilkes had paid him a compliment!

Further evidence of his quick-wittedness was the occasion on which an eminent and powerful political enemy rounded on him in public and said to him, 'You will either die of a pox or on the gallows.' Wilkes' instant response was, 'That depends, my Lord, on whether I embrace your mistress or your principles.'

DRINKING-FOUNTAINS

London grew spectacularly in the late eighteenth and in the nineteenth centuries. It did so, at least until the middle of the nineteenth century, faced with a sanitary infrastructure and water supply which were totally inadequate. The result was a host of what were coming to be called 'public health' problems. Highly contagious and sometimes lethal diseases were spread through the use of polluted water sources. There was a dire shortage of clean water and serious problems regarding the disposal of sewage. Little was known about the connection between dirt and disease. The existence of harmful pathogens invisible to the naked eye may have been suspected but was only established once technology developed sufficiently to produce microscopes powerful enough to identify them.

The prevailing political philosophy at the time was that of *laissez-faire* which argued that it was not the job of government to intervene in the economic life of the nation. If fresh clean water was needed, then private individuals or businesses would provide it, or so it was claimed. A variety of often self-perpetuating bodies, frequently of archaic origins, who were extremely jealous of their positions, were engaged in the provision of some of those services that are now known as the 'utilities'. Their efforts had never been fully adequate but the expansion of London's population was such that they were becoming wholly overwhelmed. The consequence was that London was filthy, disease-ridden, and stinking. It took decades of the nineteenth century before *laissez-faire* was seriously challenged by the radical new concept that government, both national and local, had an essential role to play in funding and providing essential public services. In the meantime, various well-intentioned individuals and a number of philanthropic bodies became involved in efforts to tackle some of the more pressing health and environmental issues.

Water has always featured in London's history. The Thames, of course, has a massive presence in the Metropolis and London, and is located where it is because throughout much of its history, it was the lowest feasible bridging point. Ancient London, huddled on the north bank of the Thames, was bounded to the west by the River Fleet and on the east by the Walbrook. It benefited by many natural springs, wells, and small streams. However, by the thirteenth century, the tributaries of the Thames and the Thames itself were basically open sewers and London faced the problem that the demand for clean water exceeded the supply. One partial solution was the building of conduits conveying water from other streams further west, such as the Tyburn, into the City. Another was a remarkable waterwheel, built in 1552, to provide the power to raise water from the Thames at London Bridge to supply the City. Further waterwheels were added later. The most complicated and expensive scheme was an artificial stream known as the 'New River'. This opened in the early seventeenth century and created a water supply using gravity from a number of natural springs in Hertfordshire to a reservoir at Islington, from whence it was piped to pumps in the City.

By the nineteenth century, London's water supply was in the hands of a number of private companies who made fortunes out of supplying seriously contaminated water to private subscribers, either through pipes to individual houses, or to standpipes accessed via a key or similar device. Those who could not afford subscriptions had to obtain their water as best they could from sources that were probably even more polluted. A few communal pumps existed but the supply was sometimes shared among thousands of local people. With its population growing from 1.1 million to 2.7 million between 1800 and 1850, London was one of the dirtiest and, from the health point of view, most dangerous cities in Europe. A rare survivor of a pump (not in use) can be found in Bedford Row, Holborn. Another is at Queen Square. Bryanston Square and Montagu Square in the West End both contain cast-iron pumps dating from the nineteenth century.

It took catastrophes to shake society out of its inertia on matters of public health. Repeated visitations of cholera between 1847 and 1854 killed over 58,000 Londoners and, more significantly so far as action taking place was concerned, this water-borne disease struck the rich and the poor with equal impartiality. Reforms backed by national and local legislation began to tackle the situation in the 1850s. Meanwhile, a number of middle-class reformers began their own intervention in what was an exceptionally dire situation. Samuel Gurney was an extremely rich MP who, in conjunction with others, formed the Metropolitan Free Drinking Fountain Association in 1859. It paid for the erection of open access drinking fountains designed to ensure that the water they provided had been filtered and was as pure as possible at the time.

The first such fountain was erected outside St Sepulchre's Church in Snow Hill but was later moved to the junction of Newgate and Giltspur Street, EC1, where it can still be seen, complete with its original cup and chain. It bears the legend 'The First Public Drinking Fountain'. Inaugurated on 21 April 1859, within a very short time the drinking fountain was being used by thousands of people daily. At the opening ceremony, the first sip of water from this exciting new facility was imbibed by the guest of honour who was none other than the daughter of the Archbishop of Canterbury. The ceremony was an occasion for rejoicing but marred a little by a tedious, rather pious, and overly long sermon by the Vicar of St Sepulchre's. The Vicar made clear in what he said that he hoped that excessive drinking and all its attendant miseries would be at least partly mitigated by the installation of large numbers of similar fountains in the near future. Many hundreds of other drinking fountains did indeed appear on or around London's streets over the next fifty years. It should be pointed out that drinking fountains had previously been erected in a handful of provincial towns and cities.

Men like Gurney may have acted on evangelical Christian principles but they were also strongly influenced by the temperance movement. Fresh, wholesome water was seen as a desirable alternative to the 'Demon Drink'. Given the shortage of safe drinking water

London's first drinking-fountain, corner of Newgate and Giltspur Streets, EC1.

plus, of course, the misery of their everyday conditions, it is hardly surprising that large numbers of working people drank to excess and that all sorts of social problems were associated with this drinking. Many drinking-fountains were deliberately sited close to public houses. The fountains often bore religious statements such as that still to be seen in Rosslyn Hill, Hampstead, NW3. This, a quote from the New Testament, reads: *Jesus said whosoever drinketh of this water shall thirst again but whosoever drinketh of the water I shall give him shall never thirst.*

The MFDFA was a solidly middle-class organisation and was aiming its efforts quite unashamedly at the manual working class who it saw as the people most likely to be in need of liquid refreshment as they moved around the Metropolis. Needless to say, they were also the people most likely to feel the need to slake their thirsts by recourse to the 'Demon Drink'. This sentiment was put into words by one of the Association's leading lights who declared, 'one saw at Cornhill eight or ten people waiting at the pump there to drink; and it struck me that fountains or pumps in the streets would save men from drunkenness.'

Close-up of the drinking cups. It is rare for an old fountain to retain these.

Over the later decades of the nineteenth century, the Association changed its character somewhat. It was initially driven by an evangelical fervour and, with its income fairly limited, the idea of the drinking fountain as being essentially a functional item with no excessive ornamentation was very much in line with the members' philosophy. It had little time for personal self-aggrandizement. However, the religious and temperance passion tended to die down over the years and many of its stalwarts, especially after 1867 when the Metropolitan Drinking Fountain and Cattle Trough Association was established, were wealthy. They wanted to ensure that if they paid for a trough or a fountain, it would be something rather striking in appearance and not easily ignored as is the way with so much street furniture, and that these structures should be as much memorials as drinking facilities. In a word, fountains became flamboyant, often being designed by leading architects. While the Association did have a standard 'cheap and cheerful' drinking fountain, many others were more about the person who financed their erection than anything to do with providing clean water for the poor or an alternative to the evils of strong drink. Brash and vulgar they may be, but where they survive they are far more likely to catch the eye than the Association's more reticent standard installations.

Greater London still has hundreds of drinking fountains although few are still able to deliver water to the weary traveller or the working man seeking escape from the alehouse. Some of them are worth mentioning. Behind the Royal Exchange in Lothbury, EC2, stand two quite exuberant fountains. One dates from 1878 and commemorates the

Drinking-fountain at the south-east corner of Lincoln's Inn Fields, WC2. This ostentatious erection posing as a drinking-fountain is really more a memorial to the memory of Philip Twells and was paid for by his wife. Twells was a nineteenth century MP.

Fire Hydrant Cover, Corfield Street, E2.

charitable work of the Draper's and Merchant Taylors' Companies. The other, a grandiose structure of marble and bronze erected in 1911, marked the fiftieth anniversary of the founding of the Metropolitan Free Drinking Fountain Association. It features a nude female figure holding a pitcher of water, although most people don't notice the pitcher. The Association was also responsible for the Wills Drinking Fountain on Blackfriars Bridge, transferred there in 1911. This also displays a female water bearer complete with pitcher although, thankfully or not, depending on point of view, this one is clothed, or at least draped.

In Old St Pancras Churchyard, Pancras Road, NW1, stands a charming prefabricated cast iron fountain manufactured by the famous Derby iron-founders, Messrs Handyside. It is based on the Choragic Monument of Lysicrates in Athens and was paid for by a well-to-do parishioner. In Albert Gardens, Stepney, E1, stands a fountain topped by a curiously clad shepherd boy carrying, for no apparent reason, a rake, sickle, and a wheatsheaf. By the Marlborough Gate of Kensington Gardens is a delightful little fountain displaying two wrestling bears. This was put up in 1939 and marks the eightieth anniversary of the Association. Lincoln's Inn Fields boasts two fountains. One, in the south-east corner, is an imposing structure placed there in 1882 by the widow of Philip Twells who had been the local MP. It has two storeys and is in a vaguely Italianate style. No one could call it beautiful. The other is less pretentious. It is in a loosely Gothic style and dates from 1861, being erected by a member of the Association but not sponsored by them. It bears the reassuring inscription – 'The Fear of the Lord is the Fountain of Life'. At the junction of Shaftesbury Avenue and New Oxford Street is a red marble fountain put up to commemorate Queen Victoria's Diamond Jubilee in 1897.

Like statues and other public commemorative items of street furniture, those fountains dedicated to the memory of particular individuals often lose some of their impact when later generations know little and care less about the person being remembered – *sic transit gloria mundi.* An example is a rather fine fountain put up in 1897 and set into the wall of the Theatre Royal in Drury Lane, WC2. This commemorates the impresario Sir Augustus Harris (1851-96). Harris may have been seen at the time as the hero whose efforts revived the fortunes of what was then the Drury Lane Theatre and indeed the cost of erecting the memorial was paid for by public subscription which would suggest that he enjoyed some real acclaim at the time. However, it would not be unfair to say that this rather grandiloquent item of street furniture, while still being *in situ,* stands to the memory of someone who is now largely, if not totally, forgotten.

In Chelsea Embankment Gardens, SW3, stands a fountain of 1887 dedicated to the memory of a man whose name lives on. This is Dante Gabriel Rossetti (1828-82). He lived close by at No.16, Cheyne Walk. This fountain is an absolute 'must-see' for fans of the Pre-Raphaelites because the bronze bust of Rossetti was the work of none other than Ford Madox Brown. On the reverse of the fountain is a list of those who subscribed financially to its erection. This includes such stalwarts of the movement as Millais, Alma-Tameda, and Holman Hunt. There's glory for you!

If ostentation and Victorian Gothic are what readers crave, then they need to go no further than Victoria Tower Gardens close to the Palace of Westminster. This fountain was originally erected close to Parliament Square but was relocated to the Gardens in 1957. It was paid for by a member of the Association in honour of his father, Sir Thomas Fowell Buxton, who had been prominent in the British anti-slavery movement. It was unveiled in 1865 to commemorate the ending of slavery in the USA when the Union finally beat the Confederates at the conclusion of the Civil War. Impressive, if architecturally eclectic, is the fountain to be seen in the Broad Walk, Regent's Park. This has to be mentioned if only because of the name of the man who paid for it. He was Sir Cowasjee Jehangeer Readymoney, an Indian Parsee grandee. He had the fountain erected in 1865 as a way of thanking the British for their treatment of the Parsee people. It was also sponsored by the Association.

FIREMARKS

The Great Fire of London of 1666 concentrated minds and led to the concept of insurance against loss or damage by fire. From around the end of the seventeenth century, companies began to provide insurance and to operate their own fire-fighting services to tackle incidents affecting the properties of their policy-holders. So that the buildings concerned could be easily identified (apart that is from the fact that they were likely to be belching forth smoke, sparks, and flames), small metal plates bearing the distinctive insignia of the insurance company were placed usually at first-floor level on the street frontages. Among the most common of these plates were those put up by the Norwich Union, Pheonix, Sun, and Britannia Insurance Companies.

Firemarks were a feature of many town houses in London occupied by those wealthy enough to be able to afford insurance, but inevitably time has taken its toll and few remain *in situ*. A number can be seen in Mount Terrace off Whitechapel Road, E1, for example, and the Museum of London, London wall, EC2, has a useful collection.

FOOTSCRAPERS

London's streets used to be notorious for their filth. Before the concept that national and local government agencies had responsibilities in the field of public health, street cleaning was in the hands of vestries and other often ad-hoc bodies which did or, in many cases, did not perform the duties which were supposed to be within their jurisdiction. Much of the filth on the streets of early Victorian London consisted of the dung produced by horses and donkeys. When the weather was wet, this just accumulated in muddy semi-solid form. During a period of consistently dry weather, the dung eventually was ground to dust, which was whirled around by passing vehicles or lifted into the air by the wind, whereupon it found its way into the eyes, ears, noses, and mouths of passers-by, and all over their clothes. It also entered any open doors and windows and settled on food and other surfaces like a lethal patina. Moving about the streets through all this ordure, especially when it was wet, meant that those who could afford them hired the services of crossing-sweepers. However, even with their ministrations, footwear soon became filthy and so footscrapers were placed close to the front doors of houses. Most of these have disappeared over the years but fine examples can be seen in Harley Street, W1. Park Street, SE1, has a good example.

Footscraper. Alley off south side of Fleet Street, EC4.

A POT-POURRI OF ASSORTED STREET FURNITURE
(PART 1)

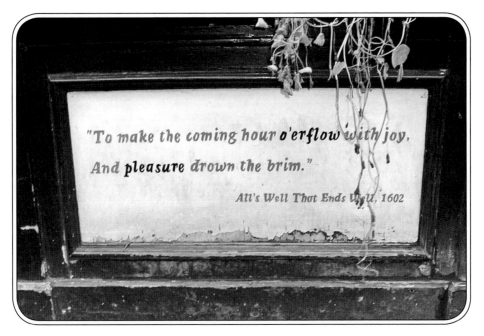

Attached to the front wall of the Seven Stars pub in Carey Street, WC2, is this sign with a Shakespearean quote. It is an eccentric touch on one of London's most eccentric pubs. Any pub with a landlady called Roxy Beaujolais has to be a bit special. The cat, a formidable feline, is called 'Tom Paine'.

Many of London's pubs display a potted history on the outside. This is the Black Lion, Hammersmith.

Lodge, Lower Temple, Victoria embankment, WC2.

No dogs at The Temple.

No dogs at Lincoln's Inn. What is it that the legal profession has against dogs?

The Lighthouse, junction of Pentonville and Gray's Inn Roads, WC1. There are many explanations for this strange building, which was erected in 1875, but no one seems to be absolutely sure. It has been semi-derelict for many years and always seems to be on the point of being regenerated, but never quite getting there.

Gibbet, Clink Street, SE1. Not a real gibbet of course, more a trade sign. The Bishops of Winchester used to have their own prison to house troublemakers who were attracted to the brothels, beerhouses, and beer gardens of Bankside. These stood on land owned by the bishopric itself. 'The Clink', as the prison was known, was burned down in the Gordon Riots of 1780. This gibbet draws attention to a museum recalling the disreputable past of the prison and its surroundings.

The Golden Boy, Giltspur Street, EC1. The Great Fire of 1666 died out at this point.

Above: Graffiti, Old Street, EC1. Adorning or blighting, depending on point of view, this particular item looks as if it has been officially sanctioned.

Right: The gates of the former Passmore Edwards Public Library, Pitfield Street, Hoxton, N1. The Library was opened in 1897, the gift of Passmore Edwards who was a rich philanthropist. The Library closed but the building now houses the Courtyard Theatre and thankfully these elegant gates have been retained.

GHOST ADVERTS

These are the remnants of old advertisements and are usually found painted on brick walls or gable ends, although occasionally they are made of inlaid letters. They may be difficult to decipher and sometimes they are at least partly covered by later advertising hoardings. Occasionally, an old shop front may contain at least part of a former advert. Few ghost signs are to be found in central London, but the south side of the west end of Fleet Street provides a not very distinct sign for the 'Aerated Bread Co.' and there is an advert for 'Black Cat Cigarettes' at Dingley Place, EC1. Weren't they the cigarettes whose advertising slogan claimed they were 'kind to the throat'? Long Acre, WC2, has a tall and thin sign advertising 'Armstrong Siddeley' and 'Connaught Coachworks'. Crispin Street, EC1, and Southwark Street, SE1, have ghost signs, but generally it is the older suburbs such as Hackney, Lewisham, Deptford, and Willesden that provide examples, although Brixton has a particularly good one for 'Bovril'. Stepney Green, E1, has a good ghost advertisement for a defunct bakery.

Old advertisements in shop doorway, Fleet Street, EC4.

Above: Incised advertisement, Portobello Road, W10.

Left: Long-obsolete brewery sign, Portugal Street, WC2. Hoare & Co., whose brewery was at East Smithfield, E1, was probably founded as early as 1492. It was taken over by Charrington & Co. in 1933 and brewing ended in 1934.

Grosvenor Works, now Gray's Antiques, Davies Street, W1.

GHOST STREET SIGNS

These are hidden away at street corners and usually consist of faded lettering, often painted on brickwork, close to the more recent and current sign. An example is Abchurch Yard, EC4, which has a City of London street name sign and, on the quoins of the building at the corner of the street above, a vaguely discernible and much older painted sign.

Quality Court, WC2.

HERALDRY

Decorative heraldry on public and private buildings is a feature of virtually every city and town and even many villages throughout England. However, it is only to be expected that it is in London that the largest variety of decorative and architectural motifs based on heraldry is to be found.

The origins of heraldry are uncertain but the concept seems to date back to the twelfth century and to have much to do with royalty, the ecclesiastical authorities, and the barons wanting to emphasise their superior positions in the social pecking order by having something conspicuous which only people of their sort were allowed to flaunt. If this definition has any substance, then it could be said that the right to display armorial bearings has much to do with status symbols. If this was true of medieval times, it is just as true today.

The tournament was just the kind of place where the red-blooded young alpha males of the ironically-named 'nobility' could get rid of some of their aggressive energy while learning the skills of combat, useful in the sort of gang warfare which we associate with the days of feudal England. The participants in the feats of arms which made up much of these tournaments wore their arms on shields, on surcoats over their armour (hence coat of arms), on helmets, etc., and even on the accoutrements of their horses. By the thirteenth century, the grandees of the time were using heraldic devices as decorations in the buildings they owned and in such things as metalwork, stained glass, and tiling. Castles, churches, palaces, houses, and tombs increasingly incorporated heraldic devices.

Royalty, in particular, liked to display its honourable lineage through the medium of heraldry. In 1290, Eleanor of Castile died in the East Midlands. She was the wife of Edward I. The King was so grief-stricken that he ordered that a memorial in the form of a stone cross should be erected at each of the overnight stopping places at which the body rested on its twelve-day journey to burial at Westminster Abbey. The last resting place was at the point later known as Charing Cross. These monuments, of course, became known as 'Eleanor Crosses' and that which can be seen close to Charing Cross Station is a Victorian replica designed to replace the original, which had been destroyed in the seventeenth century. Prominent on these crosses were the arms of England and Castile.

In the late sixteenth and early seventeenth centuries, and as a result of the Renaissance, the use of heraldry became considerably less common with the growing popularity of

Above: Heraldry at Lincoln's Inn, as seen from Chancery Lane, EC4.

Left: A heraldic symbol in a roundel at the College of Arms, Queen Victoria Street, EC4.

classical styles in architecture. However, in the humbler area of the streets, heraldic devices were frequently used to decorate shop fronts. In London, many tradesmen were engaged in such activities as engraving crests on silver or painting armorial bearings on the horse-drawn carriages of the rich. The shops, which were often effectively the fronts to their workshops, were used to advertise and to show examples of their handiwork. Sometimes, these businesses had what in effect was an endorsement from a particularly prestigious customer, such as a member of royalty or the upper echelons of the aristocracy. These have come down to modern times as royal warrants and allow the Lord Chamberlain to permit the erection of royal arms on the frontage of businesses which are recognised as the official suppliers of goods or a service to royalty. There are several old shop fronts in the St James's district of Westminster, for example, and Bond Street, Knightsbridge, and other fashionable locations in the West End.

In Queen Victoria Street, EC4, stands the College of Arms. This is the headquarters of the body having jurisdiction over every aspect of heraldry in England and Wales. The building occupies the site of the medieval London home of the powerful Earls of Derby. Two of the devices from their heraldic charge can be seen abutting onto the street.

Feudal society can be said to have ended when the barons fought themselves to a virtual standstill in the Wars of the Roses, which ended in 1485 with Henry VIII winning the throne through force of arms. The Tudor monarchs, or at least the two Henrys and Elizabeth, were great modernisers, anxious to provide the right political stability and climate in which trade, commerce, and industry could flourish. This led to the enrichment of many individuals of a bourgeois character and of a variety of guilds and corporations. They all felt that their importance entitled them to be armigerous. It was a bumper time for those who could design heraldic achievements.

Much has been said elsewhere about the so-called Gothic Revival of the late eighteenth and the nineteenth century, but one aspect of it was a harkening back to the supposedly good old days of medieval England. The Gothic villas and mock castles frequently incorporated many heraldic designs, some entirely spurious but, whether false or not, all created for effect. Public bodies also emblazoned their buildings with their arms and even humble items of street furniture such as lamp posts or bollards often displayed items of civic heraldry.

A spectacular example of this encapsulation of civic pride is provided by the boundary posts of the City of London which can be found adorning the entrances to the City via all the major roads. These consist of columns on the top of which are rather splendid heraldic dragons supporting the City's arms. Seven Dials, WC2, has the base of a former lamp standard bearing the arms of the long-defunct Holborn Borough Council.

HOLBORN VIADUCT

Holborn Viaduct is worth a section in its own right. It was completed in 1869 to cross the valley of the River Fleet and provide better road connections between the City and the West End. It is an exuberant piece of Victorian civil engineering. On the north side are bronze statues of 'Commerce' and 'Agriculture' and on the south 'Science' and 'Fine Arts'. At each corner of the viaduct are four Italianate buildings which have statues of City 'worthies' of the distant past. Lions and griffins vie for the attention of passers-by but who gives them more than a glance?

HORSE-TROUGHS

The Society for the Prevention of Cruelty to Animals was founded in 1824 and evolved into the RSPCA, founded in 1840. This had close links to the Metropolitan Free Drinking Fountain Association. The latter organisation changed its name to the Metropolitan Drinking Fountain and Cattle Trough Association in 1867. Despite its typically Victorian and extremely cumbersome title, this organisation did what it said on the tin. It erected free troughs for the refreshment of cattle, horses, and other livestock and even, in some cases, dogs. It would be nice to think that occasionally a cat came along for a drink, especially if there were no dogs about.

It was not necessary to be an avowed animal-lover to deplore the way that animals were treated on the streets of London. Until and even beyond the advent of the internal combustion engine, the horse was the prime mover of people and things on London's streets. There were hundreds of thousands of them at any one time and huge numbers of men and some women were employed as cabbies, carters, farriers, and in various associated trades. The creatures were often mistreated, neglected or horribly abused, and in some cases worked until they literally dropped dead in the shafts. They were regarded without sentiment as expendable tools. When one died or became unfit for work, it was simply replaced.

Given the nature of central London today, it is hard to visualise large numbers of animals such as cattle and sheep and even poultry being herded through the streets. That is precisely what happened, as vast numbers of these creatures that had sometimes been driven from places as far away as Wales or the Lake District made their way through the streets on the final lap of their journey to be slaughtered at Smithfield Market. In 1855, the Metropolitan Cattle Market was opened in Islington and this reduced the livestock moving through London's streets. Additionally, livestock also started being transported over the underground railway via a line into the basement of Smithfield Market and this cleared away more animals moving on the hoof along crowded streets. The drovers often cared little for the welfare of the animals supposedly in their care and it could be a distressing sight to see these tired and woebegone creatures converging on the place where they usually ended up being slaughtered. Sometimes, even in the summer, they might not be provided with water for days on end.

Cattle and horse trough, West Smithfield, EC1.

It was to address what was sometimes simply neglect, and at other times wanton cruelty, that troughs were provided, not only for animals being driven to market but also for the massive number of horses used for hauling people and inanimate cargo along London's thoroughfares. The troughs caught on. By 1885, it was estimated that over 50,000 grateful horses were using them every working day. About 500 troughs are thought to have been built on London's streets and they were, in effect, the filling stations of the equine world of the Metropolis.

After unsuccessful experimentation with materials such as iron or timber with zinc lining, which proved too vulnerable to everyday wear and tear, it became obvious that granite was the most durable and suitable material for these troughs. The MDFCTA had limited funds. Granite was expensive and so the troughs usually had the minimum of any kind of ornamentation that was superfluous to their function. However, they frequently had little aphorisms inscribed on them such as 'Be kind and merciful to animals' and 'A righteous man regardeth the life of his beast'. Sometimes, there were troughs with provision for both man and beast to quench their thirsts at the same time. The humans, we must add, were provided with cups. Such utensils were not much use for horses. At least one trough displayed a warning to the public against doing anything else with the water therein other than drinking it. This was perhaps necessary, given that it was by no means unknown for street urchins to climb into troughs stark naked to cool themselves on hot summer days.

Today, people probably find the connection between the provision of drinking fountains and the cause of temperance rather pious or self-righteous. At least one could say that the motivation behind the provision of pit-stops for horses, cattle, and other domestic creatures was solicitude for dumb animals rather than moral censoriousness.

LETTER-BOXES

The first postal pillar boxes were erected in the Channel Islands in 1852. Over the next few years, some very curious boxes put in an appearance, partly because the Post Office District Surveyors had autonomy in designing and ordering boxes, but most of them had one thing in common; they had a vertical aperture. This was thought to make it more difficult for thieves to steal items that had been posted. Be that as it may, it allowed rain to enter the box easily and frequently to cause damage to the contents.

In 1857, the powers-that-be decided that a standard box was desirable and a box with a slightly domed top and a horizontal aperture appeared. The manufacturer of the first standard design was Cochrane, Grove & Co. of Dudley and the boxes, which came in two sizes, were produced until 1866. Better-known were the 'Penfold' boxes named after their designer. Penfold boxes became a national standard and were installed between 1866 and 1879. These came in several variations but all these boxes were hexagonal, had a horizontal aperture, and an overhanging cap topped by a finial rather like a pineapple. The overhanging eaves of the cap protected the aperture from the elements, at least in theory.

Meanwhile, London had been going its own way. In 1855, a rectangular box about five feet high, having a shallow domed roof surmounted by a large iron ball, appeared in six locations in central London. The very first was at the junction of Fleet Street and Farringdon Street. These boxes were not a great success. One side of the box displayed a set of instructions at a very inconvenient height. These quickly attracted a patina of mud and other dirt, which frequently rendered them virtually unreadable. It was also felt that that this kind of box was too utilitarian for the streets of the Metropolis. In 1857-59, a box designed by Richard Redgrave of the Department of Science and Art went on trial. This more than made up in decoration for what the rectangular boxes had lacked. It was a hexagonal domed pillar of cast iron with Greek motifs and was festooned with iron mouldings in the form of flowers. Redgrave may have been a designer of beautiful artefacts but he does not seem to have been a man of very practical bent. He was so carried away with applying garlands that he forgot to include an aperture into which to put the mail! The only place they could put the aperture was in the top whereupon whenever it rained, the contents of the box got soaked. Redgrave's product was very expensive but, minus the flowery festoons and with an aperture in the right place, it was adopted as a standard pillar box in 1859.

Double pillar box, Brunswick Place, N1.

Experience convinced the authorities that a cylindrical box was best. Two boxes were designed, the A and B, differing only in their size and they became the standard until the appearance of the K in 1979. The As and Bs were a classic design, which was kept simple and functional, and they never looked outmoded. Pillar boxes had been painted in various colours in the early days but in the 1870s it was decided that all boxes should be scarlet. Not only was this an attractive colour but, of course, it rendered the boxes visible from a distance.

The double pillar box is very much an urban creature and can be found on London's streets in large numbers to deal with the bulk mail produced by the capital's financial and service industries. The first such boxes were tested out in London in 1898-9. It was known as the C box and was an immediate success, appearing in large numbers in the Metropolis. They had two apertures for what were described as 'town' and 'country' mail.

By 1978, even the As and Bs were suffering structural damage after, in some cases, decades of use. The Post Office decided that a new standard box should be brought into use. Several materials were considered, as the box needed to be able to withstand the elements, hard usage and, unfortunately, vandalism. The outcome, in 1979, was the Type K box which was a simplified, modernised version of the old standard boxes. These can be found in substantial numbers in central London as, of course, can the As, Bs and Cs. Few boxes now display the removable plate giving the time of the next collection.

Most boxes, with the exception of those made by Handyside of Derby between 1879 and 1887, have a royal cipher appropriate to the monarch on the throne at the time when the box was cast. The first of these was, of course, Victoria. For some reason, those boxes erected during the reign of George V do not bear his number. However, sometimes during repairs, doors bearing the cipher of another monarch have been used as replacements. Thus, not all boxes are what they at first seem to be. Pillar boxes have their fans and the ones they probably most want to see are those bearing the monogram of Edward VIII who was, of course, never crowned. A few can be found in London. In 1990, a more traditional-looking cylindrical box was introduced with 'Royal Mail' in embossed letters replacing 'Post Office'.

The name of the manufacturer is often found in raised letters on the black-painted base of pillar boxes.

LIGHTING

Illumination in the streets during the hours of semi or complete darkness would seem, on the face of it, a desirable and logical good idea. Not a bit of it! People have protested that darkness is God's design and who are we to tamper with it? Even in the absence of such a blatantly absurd 'argument', others have raised the issue of who should pay for such provision and why should people who never go out when it is dark have to contribute to the expense of providing a service they never use. Yet others postulated that street lighting would encourage more people out on to the streets at night, which would lead to a huge increase in drunkenness, debauched behaviour, and crime. They failed to appreciate that it was precisely the lack of lighting that was such a boon for those bent on criminal activity.

At the end of the sixteenth century, householders in London were required to display lighted candles in any windows that abutted onto the street between the hours of six and nine in the evening in the winter. Few did so. In the middle of the eighteenth century, Parliament gave the Corporation of the City of London the right to install oil lights in the streets and soon there were many thousands which provided illumination from sunset to sunrise.

Hardly qualifying as street furniture but germane to the issue of the development of public lighting in the Metropolis was the common practice, of those who could afford to do so, of hiring a link-boy or man to light them through the streets. He carried a flaming torch of burning pitch which illuminated him and those he was accompanying, but which was so bright that it rendered the surrounding darkness even more impenetrable. These lights were extinguished in the iron snuffers that, at one time, adorned the ironwork railings by the front entrance of the town houses of the well-to-do. Some elegant examples survive in Berkeley Square, W1. Others exist in parts of London and definitely qualify as street furniture.

In 1791, William Murdock, who was an employee of a Birmingham engineering company, took out a patent for the production of gas light from coal. This was a momentous step forward for mankind but it was left to a more in-your-face entrepreneur than the understated Murdock to make money out of it. This was an immigrant from Germany called Winzer who had the foresight to change his name to Winsor. He hijacked most of the understated Murdock's ideas while cleverly obscuring that fact when he set

Gas lamp,
Lincoln's Inn, WC2.

up a 'National Lighting and Heating Company', and touted shamelessly for investment funding. Winsor may have been a trifle unscrupulous but entrepreneurs do not get rich by being too fussy about doing 'the right thing'. He had drive and this was shown when, in 1807, he was given permission to demonstrate his lighting scheme by putting up thirteen gas lights in Pall Mall, close to where so many of the 'movers and shakers' of the time lived. These were successful as lighting agents although they incurred the ridicule of the satirical cartoonist Rowlandson, who sketched them with crowds passing by and making opprobrious comments. A prostitute is loudly bemoaning the fact that such lighting is bad for business.

Despite the derision, Winsor was not deterred and he went on to set up a further business, the Gas, Light and Coke Company, in 1812. He found himself on a roll and, by 1823, there were 30,000 gas lights in the streets of London alone. Some early lamps can still be seen in St James's Park, for example, in Carlton House Terrace, Trafalgar Square, Fleet Street, Temple, parts of Kensington, Westminster, especially in the vicinity of the Abbey and elsewhere. There are fine gas lamps on Westminster and Lambeth Bridges.

The nineteenth century could be called the 'Age of Cast Iron' and what might have been purely utilitarian items of street furniture often became matters of pride being elegant, artistic, and decorative. Cast iron lent itself to a very wide range of styles and

Gas lamp, Carting Lane, WC2. Waste not, want not!

Gas lamp and fine supporting bracket outside pub, Hillgay Street, W8.

designs and these attractive items went on to cast a warm, mellow, yellowish glow right across the Metropolis which was redolent of foggy nights, Hansom cabs clopping over granite setts, and Sherlock Holmes, the master-sleuth, going about his business. Miscreants look out!

Electric lights followed gas, the first probably being installed between Westminster and Waterloo, and, like gas, they were soon an everyday feature of London life. Vast numbers of either gas or electric lamps used to hang outside such places as pubs, shops, and restaurants, and were often supported by wrought iron brackets of considerable beauty. Discovering old lamps, sometimes tucked away in obscure parts of Central London, is an almost completely pointless exercise and hence a very rewarding one. The Fleet Street, Strand and Temple area are full of unexpected items of historical interest. What could be a more congenial way of spending an hour or two than walking, poking about, noting, and taking photos in this area, and then retiring to the Cheshire Cheese or any other of Fleet Street's ancient and congenial hostelries to mull over the experience with the aid of a pint or two of real ale? In fact, the Cheshire Cheese is a particularly pertinent suggestion because its entrance in Wine Office Court displays an especially large and fine globe advertising the presence of this charming establishment. Close by, fine Art Deco lamps can be seen at the former *Daily Telegraph* building, Fleet Street, and 'Unilever House', New Bridge Street, EC4.

Carting Lane, WC2, has a gas lamp, which originally, if not now, was powered by natural gas. This was long before the days of North Sea Gas, and this elegant lamp is a survivor of others that used the methane produced by the contents of sewers as the lighting agent.

MILESTONES

As with many items of furniture in the street, milestones are vulnerable. They succumb to traffic accidents, to the machinations of bureaucrats bent on widening roads and covering the UK in concrete and tarmac, or just to those other bureaucrats who lack any kind of soul and who enjoy destroying whatever is old.

London does not have many surviving milestones for the three reasons above and possibly for others. One that no longer serves its originally intended purpose is the 'Tyburn Stone', which can be seen in the window of a bank on the west side of the southern end of Edgware Road. This was a stone gatepost which originally stood by the Tyburn Tollgate, close to what is now the northern end of Park Lane. The words 'Tyburn Gate' can be deciphered and a plaque states: *This stone ... originally stood opposite the junction of Star Street and Edgware Road ... The stone is half a mile from the south end of Edgware Road where at the junction of that road with Oxford Street and Bayswater Road, Tyburn Turnpike House with three gates stood from about 1760 to 1829. Tyburn permanent triangular gallows stood from 1571 to 1759 in the position afterwards occupied by the Toll House. Tyburn was used as a place of execution from time immemorial until 1783. The first recorded execution took place in 1196.*

The London Stone set into the wall of No. 111, Cannon Street, EC4, is a fairly shapeless stone with a round top which used to be a few yards away in the wall of St Swithin's Church. It is a piece of limestone from Clipsham in Rutland and has no distinguishing marks except a pair of grooves in the top. Believed to have been located in the vicinity since about 1198, many people have argued that it is a Roman milestone. No common or garden milestone either, they say, but none other than the stone from which all distances were measured during the Roman occupation of these islands. Alternatively, it may just be a lump of stone which got there from somewhere else – origin unknown.

The 'Whittington Stone' at Highgate Hill, N6, is outside central London, but worth mentioning if only because no one really knows what it is. It stands on the west side of the road near the bottom of the hill. Supposedly, the stone marks the spot at which the disillusioned Richard (Dick) Whittington, who was trudging despondently back to his native region of Gloucestershire, heard Bow Bells chiming the unlikely refrain, 'Turn again, Whittington, thrice Lord Mayor of London.' It is believed that the stone to be seen now is the third on this site. The first possibly was the base of a preaching cross.

London Stone, Cannon Street, EC4.

Its successor was removed in 1821 when the present stone was put in place. Any real connection with Whittington is tenuous to say the least, and even the inscription on the present stone is inaccurate. Whittington was never knighted and he was Lord Mayor four times, not three as stated. Thoughtfully, a carved cat was placed on top of the stone in 1964. This was a well-deserved recognition of Whittington's great friend.

MOUNTING BLOCKS

Mounting blocks were once seen in large numbers in London, being of great utility in an age when transport was dominated by the horse. They were made of stone or bricks or occasionally of wood and usually had three or four steps. The blocks provided sufficient height to enable small or portly or not very agile people to climb easily into the saddle. Women in voluminous skirts found them a boon and they were a help to men shifting heavy loads onto carts. There are few mounting blocks left in London. A famous one stands just around the corner from the Athenaeum Club at No. 107, Pall Mall, SW1, which was for the exclusive use of the Duke of Wellington, and there is another outside the Grenadier pub in Wilton Row, SW1.

The Duke of Wellington's personal mounting block in Waterloo Place, SW1.

PLANE TREES

The London Plane, *platanus hispanica*, is an extremely common item of London street furniture. It is not indigenous to the UK but seems to have first been planted here in the second half of the seventeenth century. It is tough and resilient, long-lived, it rarely sheds its branches, will tolerate being drastically being cut back, and will seemingly flourish in poor soil even where the latter has been paved over. It has leathery leaves and these are easily washed clean by rain, and it readily used to put up with the heavily soot-laden atmosphere that was a feature of London before the Clean Air Acts. In London, plane trees account for more than half the trees to be found on the streets and in other public places and it lends a very particular character to many of London's squares. Berkeley Square, W1, has some especially large and fine examples.

A POT-POURRI OF ASSORTED STREET FURNITURE
(PART 2)

These rather nondescript stones are in Carey Street, WC2. They are generally believed to be boundary stones marking the division between two parishes.

Flood warning signs. This is the penalty for living at such a prestigious address close to the River Thames. Upper Mall, W8.

Above: Ward of Farringdon Within. Don't we just love these quaint old names?

Left: On many of the major roads into and out of the City of London, these splendid boundary markers may be seen. This one is in Moorgate, EC2.

A watch-house in Giltspur Street, EC2. This was erected to provide a base for watchmen to guard against the depredations of the 'Resurrectionists' or 'sack-'em-up men' who exhumed recently buried bodies in the churchyard of St Sepulchre's, close by. They were then sold to teachers of anatomy and surgery who used them for demonstration purposes.

Ticket machine for buses, Hoxton Street, N1. Time was when you could leap gleefully, if dangerously, on and off the open rear platform of a proper bus such as a Routemaster. You bought your ticket from a proper conductor. There was no need for such ugly machines cluttering up the pavement.

Above: Terracotta ghost shop advert for the old and revered firm of Wisden & Co. who sold cricket equipment. Leicester square, WC2. How its simple and understated style contrasts with the nondescript, even banal, sign below.

Left: Silver Jubilee Walkway, SE1. This was established in 1977 as a celebration of the Queen's Silver Jubilee. The Walkway consisted of a tour past thirty-three of London's most important and popular attractions.

POLICE BOXES

These were once familiar on London's streets. They were designed for emergency use by the public and had a light on the roof which could be flashed when the police station was trying to get in touch with an officer on patrol. They were painted blue, often made of pre-cast concrete, and the larger ones even had space for a small cell. They largely went out of use as the communications systems used by the police became more sophisticated.

Left: Hardly the Tardis! A small and careworn police box. Location forgotten.

Right: Police station, Trafalgar Square, WC2. Is this the smallest in the UK?

PORTERS' RESTS

Close to the south end of Piccadilly, W1, stands what is now a unique item of street furniture, at least as far as London is concerned. It is a porters' rest consisting of a wooden plank three inches thick supported by two cast-iron legs. It bears a plaque carrying this inscription: *This porters' rest was erected in 1861 by the Vestry of St George Hanover Square for the benefit of porters and others carrying burdens, as a relic of a past period in London's history. It is hoped that the people will aid its preservation.* Large numbers of hawkers and itinerant vendors walked London's streets crying their wares and sometimes carrying heavy loads. Just like the porters who manhandled all kinds of heavy or awkward items around the Metropolis, they would have been glad of the opportunity to lay their burden down for a few minutes at a convenient height. It seems that all the other examples of this simple device have disappeared.

Above: Postman's Park, St Martins-le-Grand, EC1. How good to see tributes to otherwise unsung heroes.

Right: Plaques in Portugal Street, WC2.

PUBLIC CONVENIENCES

The Romans had public conveniences in London, which is precisely what one would expect of these highly-civilised, if also barbaric, people. It is known that around 1291, a communal privy could be found close to London Wall, while jutting out over the Thames, near to what is now Fleet Street, was a structure with a roof and four seats. This was also a public facility, albeit likewise lacking in the privacy now thought to be so essential for us when we carry out our excretory functions. It is a pleasant thought that the roof perhaps allowed users to take their time and to admire the view even if it was raining. If there had been newspapers at the time, they might have sat down and enjoyed a good read.

A constant complaint of Londoners and visitors was the shortage of public latrines – in the fourteenth century, they seem to have averaged only one for each of the wards of the City. Things improved little, if at all, right through until the second half of the nineteenth century in spite of steeply rising demand, and it was only really when Edwin Chadwick (1800-90), the boring but zealous and persistent senior civil servant, addressed himself to the question of sanitary reform that the situation began to improve. He was aided by a benevolent monomaniac named George Jennings, who campaigned tirelessly for the provision of what he euphemistically called 'Halting Stations' in all well-frequented public places. Jennings met with much ridicule and not a little hostility in his efforts. In fact, he was probably less concerned about the sanitary aspect of things than the horrors encountered by delicate ladies and their chaste daughters, when they came across men relieving themselves openly at street corners, down alleys, and elsewhere. What must they have thought when they caught sight of such an appalling display of manhood? In all innocence, how could they have averted their eyes quickly enough when some man chose to relieve himself when they were in the vicinity? Jennings called these occasions 'sights disgusting in every sense' and he seemed to have a prurient near-obsession with the scenario. He kept returning to it.

In 1851, the Great Exhibition was staged in the Crystal Palace in Hyde Park. Jennings managed to obtain the installation of a number of conveniences. He did this despite great opposition. One can only speculate now as to why such a course of action was so controversial and what the grounds for opposition could have been. Visitors to the Exhibition could use these facilities on payment of a penny, and this novel experience lead to the emergence of the phrase 'spend a penny'. In 1852, the Duke of Wellington's funeral was held in St Paul's Cathedral. Large numbers of the supposedly great and good attended the service, and huge crowds of people lined the streets and watched proceedings around the Cathedral. Two hundred conveniences were laid on, although curiously they were only available for the gentle sex. Clearly, Jennings thought that their needs in this matter were greater than those of men. In 1855, the Crystal Palace was re-erected at Sydenham Hill in South London as what would now be called a 'leisure complex', on a very grand scale it has to be said. The obdurate Jennings persuaded the promoters to install conveniences. There was much opposition on the grounds of cost but Jennings won the day. It was found that charging a penny a time for their use meant that after an unexpectedly short period, they had more than covered the cost of their installation and upkeep and were making a profit.

The age of public health was getting under way. In 1848, a Public Health Act had required the fitting of an ash pit, a privy or a water closet to every new domestic building. In 1858, the Metropolitan Board of Works was established and Joseph (later Sir Joseph Bazalgette) began the enormous task of creating an efficient sewerage system for the rapidly-growing Metropolis. This involved the building of over 1,000 miles of superbly engineered sewers, a project which took over seven years.

Public urinals (at least this was not a euphemism) began to appear on London's streets in the 1870s. Early ones frequently contained nothing more than a long iron trough and catered only (at least in theory) for male users whose need was simply to urinate. More refined examples went on to have one or more pedestals with overhead closets and hinged seats. They became almost opulently decadent when small shoulder-high walls were used to divide the cubicles although the trough-like arrangement remained for those only wanting to urinate. Users no longer had to spend a penny.

Readers will not be surprised to learn that Jennings was at the forefront of the move to install public urinals in the streets of Britain's towns and cities. By this time he had a company which built and fitted such buildings. Other people's excretory functions proved, for him, to be the goose that laid the golden egg. It seems that he met with more resistance in London than in the provinces, but by the 1890s an increasing number of urinals or 'conveniences' were appearing on, or in many cases, under, London's streets. He made very extensive use of cast iron and usually prettified the buildings by the use of such things as finials and fancy lamps. He rarely used troughs. Instead, he employed stalls made of slate with an ingenious device which periodically flushed away the cigarette ends and other detritus dumped in them which might otherwise cause blockages. He invented the rather clever convenience which had a central pillar with the stalls around it, thus economising on space and water. Jennings produced catalogues on the front of which was a drawing showing a man emerging from one of his conveniences and adjusting his 'dress' as he did so. In the best traditions of gentle English mickey-taking, a poetaster got to work commemorating the opening of Jennings' first public convenience in London. Part of the ode went thus:

I'front the Royal Exchange and Underground
Down gleaming walls of porc'lain flows the sluice
That out of sight decants the Kidney Juice,
Thus pleasuring those gents for miles around...

Above: A surviving cast-iron lean-to urinal, Star Yard, off Carey Street, WC2.

Left: Underground toilets, Strand, WC2.

Toilets in Leather Lane, EC1. Is it just the authors who have an aversion to this kind of convenience? Is it anything to do with claustrophobia?

Good stuff, except that they were not then made of porcelain. Truly, it can be said that Jennings did for urinals what Sir Joseph Bazalgette did for sewers. They were men of the same kidney.

The cast iron conveniences erected by Jennings and others at their best are fine examples of Victorian ferrous craftsmanship. Some were circular and could cater for anything from one to four users at a time but more common were the oblong ones, free-standing or lean-to. Some were roofed but many were open to the elements. As mentioned, substantial numbers were below street level. Larger conveniences served both men and women, in separate sections, of course, and they drew attention to what they had to offer by signs marked 'Ladies' and 'Gentlemen' in a touchingly demotic way. In general, old underground conveniences are more likely to have survived, even if extensively modernised, than those on the streets.

As with so much street furniture, traffic accidents and road widening have taken their toll of urinals. A rather nice decorative cast-iron facility stands in Star Yard, Chancery Lane, WC2. It is not in use. An underground urinal with separate sections for men and women and similarly not in use can be found in Holborn, EC1.

PUB SIGNS

Pub signs and names provide marvellous insights into the history of London, often in particular to quirky or forgotten aspects of that history. Like shop signs, pub signs date back to the age of large-scale illiteracy where an easily-distinguished emblem or symbol would inform people on the streets of the nature of the business carried on in any particular premises.

The Romans had little time for ale, being avid fans of wine and they caroused in drinking houses called 'tabernae' from which the modern word 'tavern' is derived. They advertised the presence of the tabernae by a display of greenery, often vine leaves, perhaps attached to a pole jutting out from the front of the building. It is probable that early alehouses in England displayed a sign of a similar kind, if not actually of vine leaves, and this would explain the considerable number of pubs with names like The Vine or The Grapes. Over time a new kind of sign evolved which was the painted board, perhaps attached flat on the wall or increasingly swinging on the top of a free-standing pole close to the building. A later kind of sign of which London once had several was that known as a 'gallows sign'. This stretched at some height across the street and was supported by the buildings on either side. A signboard might be attached to this or some sort of three-dimensional representation of the name of the drinking house.

Pub signs and names tend to lend themselves to being placed into convenient categories and a few of these will be considered below, with the proviso that change is happening so fast in the hospitality industry that it is quite impossible to ensure that information is right up-to-date. Pubs are closing at a seemingly growing rate while many of those that survive undergo a change of name and identity, not very often for the better.

FAMOUS PEOPLE

JOHN SNOW, Broadwick Street, Soho, W1. Perhaps this sign refers to someone who is not as famous as he perhaps deserves to be although it is unlikely that he was the kind of man who sought celebrity. Snow was a doctor who studied statistics relating to an outbreak of cholera in the Soho district in 1854. The mortality was greatest among those who used a particular pump as their water supply. From this he deduced that the water must have been contaminated by what he and other medical men and scientists were beginning to believe were microscopic disease-bearing pathogens. Many people at the time thought that such an idea was perfectly outrageous, but he went ahead and boldly removed the device which activated the pump. The locals were forced to go elsewhere for their water supplies and mortality dropped dramatically. Q.E.D. The pub with its unique name stands close to where the pump was. A plaque provides an explanation.

MARQUIS OF GRANBY. London has a few houses of this name. It recalls John Manners (1721-70), a senior army officer who gained respect because, unlike some other commanders who skulked behind while ordering others to their deaths, he led literally from the front. He also recognised the loyalty of long-serving petty officers under his command and often bought them pubs so that they had a future after they had left the colours. The popularity this brought him is reflected in the pub name because some of the ex-soldiers renamed the pubs they took over as a tribute to him. Three pubs with this name are in Dean Bradley Street, SW1, Chandos Place, WC2, and Rathbone Street, WC1.

ANIMAL SIGNS

COCKPIT, St Andrew's Hill, EC4. The sign shows fighting cocks and refers to what is now considered a barbaric 'sport'. Cocks were bred for strength, endurance, and aggression and armed with steel spurs which could inflict appalling injuries. A prize bird could be a lucrative investment for its owner. A famous print by Hogarth called 'The Cockpit' depicts the squalid and frenzied scene at a cockfight where fortunes could be lost and won on the outcome of each bout. Cock-fighting was outlawed in 1849, but has never completely died out in some rural parts of Britain.

HORSE & GROOM. One pub with this name is in Great Portland Street, W1. The name and the signs outside recall the fact that this was a very prestigious residential area of London occupied by 'carriage folk'. Horses hauled them as they went through the streets and substantial numbers of servants were needed to look after the horses and their accoutrements and the carriages and conveyances. A pub with the same name is tucked away in Groom Place, SW1, which is a mews serving the same kind of residential area.

RELIGIOUS SIGNS

BISHOP'S FINGER. This can be found close to Smithfield Meat Market in EC1. A bishop raises his finger in what looks like a blessing rather than in admonition. In some country districts, a 'bishop's finger' was a signpost usually placed at a road junction. Irreverent people sometimes refer to this pub as 'The Nun's Delight'.

BLACK FRIAR, Queen Victoria Street, EC4. One of London's most eccentric pubs is a curious, wedge-shaped building just to the north of Blackfriars Bridge. Its main external sign is a three dimensional, podgy, and cheerful-looking monk. Inside the pub, which is a masterpiece of art nouveau decoration, are innumerable plump and amiable monks happily pursuing a range of hedonistic pleasures accompanying their activities with amusing observations on life. An establishment of the Dominicans or Black friars used to stand close by.

CURIOUS SIGNS

BARROW BOY & BANKER, Borough High Street, SE1. This unique name can be taken in different ways. It stands close to the south end of London Bridge which links the City's financial institutions with Southwark where Borough Market is still a significant presence. It might, of course, be taken as a wry comment on both barrow boys and bankers as being the kind of people who will pull a fast one if they can, the difference being that the bankers do it with much larger amounts of other people's money and accrue correspondingly greater profit.

CARTOONIST, Shoe Lane, EC4. This pub is unique in two ways. It is the only one with this name and the only one with a sign which changes annually. The Cartoonists' Club is based here and it holds an annual competition for the best new sign. The winner then takes pride of place, being exhibited outside the pub for the following year. Examples of previous winners can also be viewed outside the building.

DIRTY DICK'S, Bishopsgate, EC2. This recalls the story of Nathaniel Bentley, whose life fell apart when he was jilted by his fiancée on the eve of their wedding. He couldn't cope and became a recluse who refused either to wash himself or make any attempt to clean his surroundings, which over the years became covered in filth. On his death, many of his possessions were bought by a publican who used them as props for his theme pub. The pub became known as 'Dirty Dick's' after this particular landlord and it had many dirty-looking artefacts on show, including such things as dusty old violins and the skeletal remains of long-dead cats. Dirt-encrusted cobwebs were everywhere. Unfortunately, the heavy hand of Heath and Safety was brought to bear on this engaging collection of detritus and little remains except the name.

FRIEND AT HAND, Herbrand Street, WC1. This is a rare name. The sign currently shows a man literally up to his neck in snow, being approached by a benevolent but rather soppy-looking St Bernard, complete with a barrel of brandy round his neck. It is only to be hoped that a rescue was completed successfully.

HUNG, DRAWN & QUARTERED, Great Tower Street, EC3. To be grammatically pedantic, this should be 'hanged' rather than 'hung', but anyway here is a unique and interesting sign. This appalling punishment was usually reserved for those found guilty of treason. The condemned felon was drawn on a hurdle to the site of the execution. He or she was then hanged, but only enough to achieve partial strangulation, while remaining partly conscious. Then the victim was cut open and eviscerated. If the victim was male he would probably also be castrated at this stage, the idea being to demonstrate that he could father no more traitors in the future. The bowels and entrails were then burned while

Leather Exchange pub sign, Leathermarket Street, SE1. Signs such as this provide marvellous insights into local economic and industrial history. Such names should not be changed at the whim of some half-baked marketing whizz-kid.

the victim was encouraged to look on. He did not have too long to ponder on the sight because he was then beheaded and quartered. This meant that the torso was chopped roughly into four parts, which were then usually displayed on the gates of the City as a dire warning about how other traitors would be dealt with. At the place of execution, the ritual ended with the executioner holding up the severed head of the victim and uttering the immortal words, 'Behold, the head of a traitor! So die all traitors!'

INTREPID FOX, Wardour Street, W1. The name of this pub refers to Charles James Fox (1749-1806). He was the stormy petrel of parliamentary politics, perhaps best remembered for his opposition to slavery and tolerance towards Catholics and Nonconformists. He was a rake, avidly drinking, womanising, and gambling and something of a popular figure with the populace. The landlord of the pub was one of his greatest fans.

SHIP & SHOVEL, Craven Passage, Charing Cross, WC2. The name is unique and the pub is unique because it has two separate parts on either side of the passage. Sir Clowdisley Shovel or Shovell (1659-1707) was a distinguished admiral in the Royal Navy, who was on his way back to England from a successful tour of duty in the Mediterranean when several ships of his squadron were blown off course onto the Bishop and Clerk Rocks

Pawnbroker's brass balls, Castle pub, Cowcross Street, EC1. This is the only pub additionally licensed to act as a pawnbroker, hence the characteristic sign. An heir to the English throne, regretfully we have to say, a man of somewhat dissipated character, had gambled all his money in the nearby flesh-pots, but obtained the money for a cab ride back home by pledging his fine watch with the landlord of the Castle who did not know who he was. Next morning, the Prince sent his servant to redeem the watch with a licence signed to the effect that the pub was now able to act as a pawnbroker in perpetuity.

close to the Scilly Isles, where they were wrecked. Shovell, who was extremely corpulent, was swept into the sea and washed ashore, largely unhurt. Exhausted and soaked and lying exhausted on the sand, he must nevertheless have been thanking his lucky stars when he was approached by a local woman who would surely provide him with succour. It was not to be. She spotted a large emerald ring on his finger and promptly murdered him in order to wrench it off his finger. It is said that she hit him with a shovel. This latter part of the story may be apocryphal.

THE RUNNING FOOTMAN, Charles St, W1. Running footmen were employed by rich men in the eighteenth century. They were dressed in their master's livery and they ran some distance ahead of his carriage to warn wayside inns to provide new horses and/or hospitality. They also paid the tolls on turnpikes so that the master's carriage did not have to stop to pay them. The story goes that this smart part of London had many running footmen employed in the big houses and that they probably used this pub which consequently became known as 'The Running Footman'. One day someone who knew about such things went in and told the landlord that the name of his pub was unique and ever since the sign has borne the legend, 'I am the Only Running Footman'.

THREE KINGS, Clerkenwell Close, EC1. This small and quirky pub has a fairly common name which refers to the Three Wise Men from the East who supposedly came to the cowshed in which Jesus was born in Bethlehem, bearing gifts for the infant, recognising that he was someone special. There is nothing commonplace about the sign which manages to combine three other 'kings'. They are Henry VIII, which is fair enough, Elvis Presley, and King Kong. The inside is equally eccentric and definitely worth a look. This sign was missing on a recent visit to Clerkenwell.

WALRUS AND THE CARPENTER, Lower Thames Street, EC3. A unique name in London, this refers to the characters in the surreal *Alice in Wonderland* by Lewis Carroll. They were walking on the beach (possibly that stretching northwards from Whitby to Sandsend in North Yorkshire) and were weeping like anything to see such quantities of sand. They pretended to befriend some oysters by taking them for a walk, only to eat them with bread and butter, pepper, and vinegar.

PUMPS

Before the second third of the nineteenth century, large numbers of Londoners derived most, if not all, of their water from communal pumps. As late as the 1840s, 30,000 Londoners did not even have access to piped water dispensed through such pumps. Where pumps existed, the supply was frequently erratic or restricted to a brief period and only available to subscribers who had the right keys to gain access. The East London Waterworks Company, for example, did not supply water on Sundays and on weekdays only between 4.35 and 4.55 in the morning or 7.10 and 7.25, also in the morning. Many of the 30,000 luckless Londoners mentioned above took all their water from butts which stored unfiltered rainwater. The body of a decomposing baby was once found in one of these.

Most of London's pumps have disappeared but examples can still be found at Cornhill and Aldgate, both in EC3 and Bedford Row, WC1. Conduits formerly existed in some numbers, usually being large well heads often elaborate enough to be described as 'architecture'. They are remembered now only in such street names as White Conduit Street, N1, Conduit Place, W2, and Lamb's Conduit Street, WC1.

Right: Pump on north side of St Paul's Churchyard, EC4.

Below: Also in St Paul's Churchyard is this exhortation to the public who like to share their sandwiches with their feathered friends.

RAILINGS

Doubtless, railings have their devotees. The authors may be nerds, but this is one item of street furniture that even they cannot get excited about. Many fine examples of old railings can be found in such areas as St James's, Mayfair, and Regents Park. When we were children we heard all about the drive to uproot railings to produce scrap iron to assist the war effort in the early 1940s. We suspect that railings were seized and removed more keenly from working-class districts of London than from the fronts of the houses of people who had wealth and social and political clout in such places as those mentioned above.

In Harleyford Street, SE11, near The Oval, is a unique set of railings composed of wartime ARP stretchers.

Lampposts, trees, and dogs are synonymous. This will frustrate the blighters.

SHOP FRONTS
AND SHOP SIGNS

In medieval England, the bulk of retailing was carried out in markets and fairs or goods were purchased from itinerant traders. Early shop fronts were very simple, consisting of a door and a window. One shutter would act as a primitive display unit while the other would provide a basic canopy. Transactions were conducted through the window.

We know that shop fronts of a somewhat more modern style were in use in the seventeenth century. One such was at Temple Bar and was demolished in 1846. Others on record were at Fenchurch Street in the City and Macclesfield Street in Soho. They have also disappeared. In Cheapside, in what is now EC2, the south side of the street consisted almost completely of goldsmiths' shops and this constituted a sight which foreign visitors to London always wanted to see. These businesses moved on to what is now the Hatton Garden area of Holborn, and they were replaced by a wide variety of dealers in other commodities.

In the eighteenth century, a recognisable shop front began to evolve. It emerged from existing domestic premises and it was the street frontage of these which determined their size, since they were largely restricted to the space between the party walls of the buildings on either side. A large and heavy beam, inserted in the front of the building above the ground floor, held up the front of the building and allowed the insertion at street level of a framework containing small windows, which enabled the wares on offer to be displayed. This, it was hoped, would entice customers into the shop. Another feature of these shops was their hanging signs. These were almost universal and were very varied and often large and elaborate. In such large numbers, they constituted a hazard for people using the street, especially those on horseback. They also blocked out air and sunlight. Sometimes lack of maintenance caused them to fall on passers-by. In 1762, an order was passed requiring those in the City to be removed. Westminster followed suit not long after.

Hanging shop signs were very like their counterparts advertising inns, taverns, coffee houses, and other drinking places. In many cases, they had heraldic motifs, but there were royal insignia, fabulous beasts, and many other features, all intended to catch the attention with a striking visual image in a time of mass illiteracy. In 1710, a wry little verse was penned about the strange incongruities that occurred in the signs that sometimes brought together very diverse or sometimes seemingly incompatible themes:

I'm amazed at the Signs
As I pass through the Town
To see the odd mixture;
A Magpie and Crown,
The Whale and the Crow,
The Razor and Hen,
The Leg and Seven Stars,
The Axe and the Bottle,
The Tun and the Lute
The Eagle and Child,
The Shovel and Boot.

Various trades adopted more-or-less standard motifs for their signs. Examples include Bell Founders – Three Bells; Button Makers – Golden Lion; Clog Makers – Patten & Crown; Coopers – Bathing Tub and Pail; Grocers – a Golden Canister or a Fig Tree or Three Sugar Loaves; Leather Sellers – Roebuck; Musicians – Tabor and Pipe; Robe Makers – Bishop's Head or Parliament & Judges Robes; Silk Weavers – Blue Boar and lastly Tailors – Drayman and a Jacket, Golden Fleece or Hand & Shears.

Shop signs would once have been as common as pub signs but few are still to be seen, particularly in Central London. Spectacular ones can be seen in St James's Street, SW1. These are carved Native Americans, the traditional symbol of tobacconist's shops, and these do indeed grace the outside of old-fashioned and prestigious cigar merchants. A unique sign is to be found on the front of the Castle pub in Cowcross Street, EC1. This is the three brass balls indicating a pawnbroker's business. The Castle is the only pub in Britain also licensed to act as a pawnbroker. The story goes that George IV, a wastrel of the first order, was out one night slumming it incognito in the flesh-pots of the City. He had lost money gambling and could not afford the cab fare home. He went into the Castle and managed to obtain a loan from the landlord, leaving his magnificent watch as a pledge. Next morning, he sent a footman to redeem the watch and to present the landlord with a royal warrant allowing him and his successors in perpetuity to conduct a pawnbroking business on the premises.

From the middle of the eighteenth century, Britain was entering into the era conveniently, if a trifle misleadingly, called the Industrial Revolution. This process, which in a sense has never stopped, is however usually thought of as ending around 1850. It involved, among other things, a massive increase in the amount of wealth generated within the economy and the very considerable enrichment of some sections of society, even if it meant poverty and misery for many others. London was the commercial, financial, administrative, legal, and cultural centre of Britain and it housed large numbers of the rich and middling orders who had considerable spending power and money to spare for what are now called consumer goods, which were items bought for pleasure or self-gratification rather than necessity. The presence of these consumers and the serving of their rising expectations led to a considerable expansion of the retail industry in the Metropolis. To attract customers, shops needed to pay considerable attention to their appearance and state-of-the-art methods of display.

The bow window enjoyed several decades of popularity, offering as it did opportunities for the best display of goods, making the maximum use of the space available and of

Left: Shop sign, Jermyn Street, SW1.
Right: Shop sign, Strand, WC2.

natural light. However, in 1774, local legislation considerably restricted the acceptable size of the protrusions made by the bow windows. Some of the shop fronts dating from the eighteenth century are fine examples of the work of the carpenters and glaziers of the time, but an architectural purist would deny them much merit.

Early shops had shutters which were taken down and stored in preparation for business and replaced when the shop closed, a task unpopular with the apprentices usually charged with doing it. Very few shops with shutters are still to be seen. In the 1840s, iron roller shutters were introduced and roller blinds about the same time. These provided shade for the protection of the goods on display in the shop window, but there were many complaints in the early days about those with side aprons which were so low that they conflicted with the movement of pedestrians along the pavement.

A French visitor to London in the mid-1820s contrasted the cheerful and bright lights and displays of the shops with their drab and soot-encrusted surroundings. No city in Britain was as sooty as London, with the possible exception of Edinburgh. The miasmic murk which is made so much of by Conan Doyle in the Sherlock Holmes stories was every bit as much a reality for Londoners as 'Auld Reekie' was for the citizens of Edinburgh. Gas lighting appeared for the first time in the 1790s and those shopkeepers who could afford it adopted gas with great enthusiasm to catch the eye and give the impression that they were on the cusp of the latest technological advances. Effective lighting was necessary anyway, because the shops of central London tended to be open until nine or even ten o'clock at night. Many shops in Oxford Street, for example, provided a warm and welcoming blaze of light to catch the attention of potential customers. Woburn Walk in

Shop front, Smith & Sons, New Oxford Street, WC1.

St Pancras, WC1, gives a good idea of a parade of early nineteenth century shops before the arrival of the larger emporia that became a feature of several parts of London during the nineteenth century. A shop front of about 1820 acts as a façade for the Whitechapel Bell Foundry in Whitechapel Road, E1. It is a remarkable survivor.

Paris always had the style and the chic and contained covered walks or arcades of shops which were first copied in Britain in the Royal Opera Arcade joining Pall Mall to Charles Street, W1. It was designed by John Nash and G.S. Repton and contained a number of small specialist luxury shops. It was completed in 1818 and was followed the next year by Burlington Arcade off Piccadilly, W1. Designed by Samuel Ware for Lord Burlington, this also had shops aimed at a wealthy clientele and also served to prevent passers-by throwing rubbish, including wrappers of take-away food, into the good Lord's garden.

Time has not been kind to the eighteenth and nineteenth century shop fronts of London. The growth of the retail sector and the outright competition that was created had little time or sentiment for the shopkeeper who would not move with the times unless it was in the prestigious end of the market. This sector positively encouraged the sense of vintage provenance, tradition, and continuity and there are still shops in London's West End that trade on this concept.

Developing technology in the 1840s enabled the manufacture of much larger pieces of glass and the plate-glass window began to appear around that time. This allowed far larger displays which in turn was part of the drive to the provision of larger shops, particularly in the prestigious retail areas of the West End. On a more modest scale, there

Shop front, Harvie & Hudson, Jermyn Street, SW1.

Shop fronts, Woburn Walk, WC1. These well-preserved frontages give us some idea of the small scale but attractive appearance of what would have been shops for the well-to-do.

Above: Sicilian Avenue.
A more modern version
of Woburn Walk, it was
completed in 1910.

Right: Sign for a fishmonger's
shop, Kensington Church
Street, W8.

Barclay's Bank sign, Fleet Street, EC4. This sign used to be a familiar one up and down the country. One day they were there and then re-branding took place and they disappeared.

Truman's Black Eagle, Brick Lane, E2. Still to be seen outside what was Truman, Hanbury & Buxton's Brewery in Whitechapel, the Black Eagle was once a trade mark familiar in many parts of London.

are some fine fronts of the 1850s employing wooden frames and large panes of sheet glass in Museum Street, Bloomsbury, WC1.

What is meretricious for one generation may become a tasteful idol for later ones. A very fine example of an extremely showy frontage of the 1870s is the umbrella shop of James Smith and Sons at No. 53, New Oxford Street, WC1. It attracts the attention of passers-by because it is such an anachronism. It has a mass of coloured lettering painted on the back of glass and lettering on its brass fascia plates. At one time the main shopping streets of London would have been full of shop-fronts of this sort, but they fell very rapidly out of fashion after the First World War. This one has almost achieved cult status.

Still exuberant, but rather more tasteful, is No.117 Mount Street. This employs much terracotta, dates from 1886, and was in a district in which the Duke of Westminster rather feudally laid down the law about the appearance of the buildings erected on his land. Elegant shops employing substantial amounts of dark glass or polished woodwork can be found at No. 123, Cheapside and No. 67, Moorgate, both in the City. These date from around 1900.

Some other interesting fronts are the Savoy Taylors' Guild of 1903 in the Strand; Sicilian Avenue off Southampton Row, 1905; 14-16 New Cavendish Street, 1902; Hatchard's, Piccadilly of 1912 and, in a loosely Art Deco style, Ganolphi Ballet shoemakers at No. 150, Marylebone High Street, and at No. 118, London Wall, Fox's, the umbrella and walking stick retailer with a superb black vitriolite façade of about 1935.

STREET SIGNS

Street signs provide a distinctive landmark in London and often reflect changes as well as historical associations. The Victorian passion for regulating and bringing order by renaming streets made it difficult to trace an exact location in the past. In 1811 the *Gentleman's Magazine* noted that the 'practice of giving new names to streets appears ... very absurd ... it tends to make confusion, and lead people into mistakes.'

Before the nineteenth century, street names were mainly generic and descriptive, usually named after the goods sold in them such as Bread Street. Thereafter it was common for streets to bear the name of eminent individuals from British history or some local dignitary. Some street names have been corrupted over the centuries and have less obvious roots. The first major street renaming scheme was started in 1857 by the Metropolitan Board of Works (MBW), encouraged by the General Post Office. Further changes took place in the 1890s, after the London County Council (L.C.C.) was formed to replace the MBW and again between 1929-1945. Evidence of older signs can still be seen. Some older names, such as Pissing Alley (and this is one of the milder ones) no longer exist – clearly too sensitive for modern sensibilities.

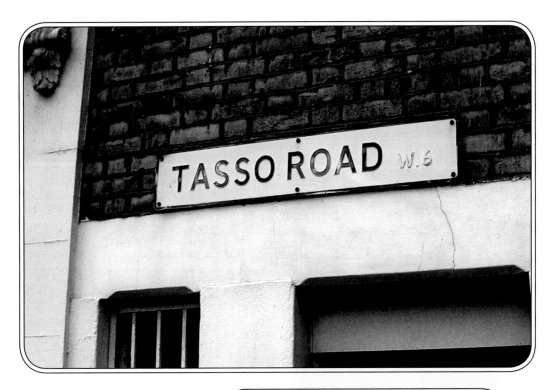

Above: Tasso Road, W6. Just one of many suburban streets named after someone now forgotten.

Right: Sclater Street, E1. This is one of the very oldest street signs in London.

A survivor of an older style of sign. W8.

This sign recalls the fact that coal, usually from Northumberland and Durham, came down the east coast in tough little collier ships. It was then transferred to barges and brought up the River Fleet to be unloaded and distributed to consumers in the City, hence the earlier name. The limeburners themselves would have made use of this coal.

Rabbit Row, W8. There is a world of history in London's street names. Strange though it may now seem for somewhere so close to Notting Hill, this area was once riddled with rabbit warrens and a brisk business was done catching bunnies and selling them for the cooking pot.

SUNDIALS

Our lives are governed by time. Most of us carry a timepiece around and spend half the day looking anxiously at our wrists in the hope that we're not falling behind on the commitments we have made or fretting about why the bus is two minutes late.

Our ancestors had a more relaxed attitude to time. One-handed clocks were perfectly adequate for most of a slower-moving society's needs, and sundials gave an indication of time even if they had the drawback of not being much use in the hours of darkness or when the sun was not shining. Many sundials were set up vertically attached to walls in public places where they could easily be seen. Others could be found carved into the stonework of buildings or often on the top of pillars.

One of the best-known is that at Seven Dials, WC2. This is actually a replica of an earlier pillar on the same site which was demolished in 1773 because it acted as a gathering place for 'undesirables', there being many of these in this district which was one of London's most notorious criminal 'rookeries'. Its replacement actually has only six dials but is something of a landmark for all that. It was unveiled in June 1989 by Queen Beatrix of the Netherlands as part of celebrations to mark the three-hundredth anniversary of the accession to the throne of William of Orange and Mary Stuart. Set into a ring at the base of the steps is a list of the benefactors who contributed to the cost of its erection.

Other sundials are the small ornamental horizontal ones, which can often be found in parks. Although rather out of Central London, a number of sundials can be seen at the Royal Observatory, Greenwich. The Church of St Margaret, Parliament Square, SW1, has interesting modern vertical dials on the four faces of its west tower.

TELEPHONE BOXES

Telephone services started in Britain in the late 1870s. At that time, telephones could only be used by people who paid a subscription to a provider, the dominant one being the National Telephone Company (NTC). In 1884, non-subscribers could use the service on a 'pay-as-you-go' basis. This could be done from 'call offices'. These were frequently inside shops whose proprietors hoped to lure customers in to make a call whereupon they might be persuaded to make additional purchases. (Rather like cash-dispensing machines these days). With increasing use of telephones, call offices appeared at such places as post offices and railway stations. Call offices in the street were introduced around 1900, some being manned by a company employee, but increasingly they became coin-operated. Early call offices were made of wood and came in a variety of designs.

The NTC operated by the far the larger part of the British telephone system, but it was nationalised in 1896 and, from 1911, the General Post Office took over all existing telephone networks except those provided by the local authorities of Portsmouth and Hull. Portsmouth was soon subsumed by the GPO, but Hull's telephone system has remained independent to the present time. With what was basically one national network, there was soon a drive for standardisation and what would now be called a 'house style'. The favoured design for what we will now call the 'kiosk' was that known as the 'Birmingham'. This was remarkably similar to some modern telephone boxes except for its overhanging eaves and low pyramidal roof topped by a cute finial. It was constructed of wood and appeared in many different colours.

In 1921, there appeared the prototype of what it was hoped would become a national standard telephone box. This was Kiosk No. 1. It was rather like a reinforced concrete updated version of the Birmingham Box. Although it was accepted in some places, the local authorities of most of the London boroughs took an immediate dislike to it, largely because they thought it obstructed the pavement. The outcome was the holding of a competition. As well as a consideration of existing designs, a small number of leading architects were invited to put forward a design for a standard kiosk that would be made of cast iron and would cost no more than £40. The public were asked to indicate which they favoured and the design that met with most approval was that submitted by Giles Gilbert Scott. This box began to appear on the streets of London and elsewhere in 1926. Not surprisingly, it was designated 'Kiosk 2', soon shortened to 'K2'. The exterior

K2 Telephone box, Red Lion Court, EC4.

was painted vermilion and the interior 'flame'. It managed to look both elegant and businesslike. Scott's kiosk had a domed roof, pierced crowns in the tympani, and was pleasing in its simplicity. The problem was that the K2 was expensive and too big, and so for a while modified versions of the K1 continued to be installed in large numbers. What the authorities wanted was a combination of K1 and K2 which was small, cheap, and stylish. The outcome was, predictably, the K3. It was introduced in 1929, was made of concrete, was very similar in appearance to the K2, and became the country's standard phone kiosk, being produced in huge numbers. The K2, however, despite its bulk, became particularly characteristic of London and rare in the provinces.

In 1927, a jumbo-sized box, the K4, had made its appearance. It seems as if the Post Office was seeking to cut down on the cost of providing and staffing main post offices because this was a mini-post office intended to provide a service in the street. It trebled as a phone box, a post box, and a post office by virtue of having a coin-operated machine dispensing stamps. It was sometimes referred to officially as the '24-hour post office'. This behemoth was basically a stretched K2, being about half as large again and there weren't many pavements that were large enough to be reasonably able to accommodate it. It was very expensive as well as a serious obstruction to the flow of pedestrians and very few of them were built. Complaints were frequently voiced that anyone using the phone was deafened when someone used the stamp machine and also that, especially when it was raining, the stamps got wet and stuck to each other when they were dispensed.

The K5 introduced in 1934 was a curious aberration. It was designed to be assembled quickly and dismantled equally quickly and to be used particularly at short-term events such as exhibitions. It is unlikely that any of these ever appeared on London's streets.

It became apparent that concrete phone boxes were something of a false economy because, while the cost of their installation was initially cheaper, they needed more expensive maintenance than cast-iron boxes. When it was decided to design a new box as part of the celebrations around the Jubilee of King George V, not surprisingly, it was designated K6 and often called the 'Jubilee Kiosk'. This was cast-iron, it was painted red, it was somewhat slimmed down, and it proved to be the classic British phone box, there being eventually over 60,000 installed in the UK, with thousands on London's streets. As well as sometimes being in entirely new locations for phone boxes, the K6 replaced large numbers of K1s and K3s. K6s were still being installed well into the 1960s, being the standard kiosk from 1936 to 1968. It is thought that as many as 900 K6 boxes are listed 'buildings'.

In 1962, the K7 made a limited appearance. The Post Office had decided that a more modern-looking box, which was cheap to install and maintain, was needed. Designs were submitted and the one chosen had an aluminium frame and more glazing than any previous boxes. A group of three was installed in Grosvenor Gardens, SW1. The Post Office did not proceed with the K7. The K8 was the outcome of a competition held in 1965. It had a cast iron body with an aluminium door and extensive glazing and made its public debut in London in 1968. Many K6s had their glazing bars ripped out so that they had a single pane of glass on each side like a K8.

It could be said that the day of the classic phone box was now over. Boxes, like other public installations, were increasingly being subjected to neglect, abuse, and deliberate vandalism. Issues about access were being considered more pertinent and demanded

Above: K2s and K6s huddle together for company.

Right: Trompe L'Oeil, Eagle Place, SW1. A clever optical illusion.

radical new approaches to how kiosks were designed. Glass was expensive but when it was replaced by polycarbonate that couldn't be easily broken, it was found that the vandals took to inscribing graffiti on it instead. The windows could eventually become more or less opaque. Such kiosks were extremely uninviting. With this in mind, the 'Booth 7A' appeared in the early 1980s. This was an open-fronted walk-up booth on a stout pedestal and painted bright yellow.

In 1985, the 'KX' range of boxes was introduced. Of these, the most common was the KX100 which is recognisably a descendent of previous classic designs. Also appearing on the streets were the KX200, which was a unit with a listening hood, and the KX300, which was triangular and designed to be part of a cluster of kiosks. The KX410 and 'KX420' were phones on posts and not kiosks. Handier for access some of these may have been, easier to maintain, and more difficult to vandalise, but none of them captured the public imagination like the classic kiosks. People clearly hankered after the past and so British Telecom introduced the 'KX Plus' which basically consisted of a KX100 with a domed red roof and a red bar round the side. There has even been a KX Plus kiosk with internet facilities, which was not a great success.

From the 1990s, with deregulation in the telecommunications industry, a number of other companies appeared on the scene to challenge BT's place in the market and they have introduced kiosks and boxes in a variety of colours and styles. British Telecom has seen its income from payphones fall dramatically in the twenty-first century with the almost universal ownership of personal mobile phones, and there is little doubt that telephone kiosks are disappearing rapidly from London's streets. Such is the public affection at least for the earlier iconic designs that small numbers of preserved kiosks are likely to be a feature of London street furniture into the foreseeable future.

The K2s and K6s were perfect examples of how something as utilitarian as street furniture can be both functional and beautiful at the same time.

WELLS

Central London stands on the flood plain of the Thames as it meanders its way towards the sea. This provides a thin layer of rich soil in places but all Londoners who are gardeners know, and often rue the fact, that underneath the alluvium is a thick layer of resistant and non-porous clay which is exceptionally difficult to work. Less obviously beneath that is a layer of porous chalk. In places where the clay is particularly thin, streams come to the surface and form tributaries to the Thames. Most of these streams are now largely underground and the Fleet, for example, makes a valley wide and steep-sided enough that Holborn Viaduct had to be built across it to join the City with the Charing Cross area and Westminster. The names of these streams are remembered in such street names as Fleet Street, EC4, Cranbourn Street, WC2, Tyburn Way, W1, and Walbrook, EC4.

Not just small rivers came up to the surface, but also springs and wells. Holywell Lane and Holywell Row in EC2 are situated close to the former Holywell Priory in Shoreditch on the site of an ancient sacred well. Some of these springs were exploited as spas in the eighteenth and nineteenth centuries and Sadler's Wells Theatre, for example, recall the wells around which a very prosperous pleasure garden once flourished. Bottles of this supposedly health-giving water can be bought at the theatre. Apparently, they come from the theatre's own borehole. Clerkenwell is a reminder of another former well close by and, indeed, in Farringdon Lane it is possible to view part of the old well through a basement window. There are several premises in London which benefit from their own wells. These include Harrods and the Bank of England.

A POT-POURRI OF ASSORTED STREET FURNITURE
(PART 3)

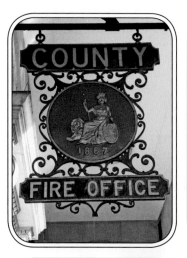

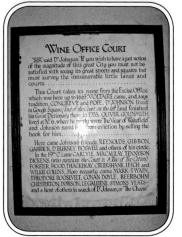

Dolphin Lamppost in close proximity to camel benches on the Victoria Embankment, WC2.

Light Extinguisher, St James's Square, SW1. Before the days of street lighting, men could be hired to light the way. When they reached the destination, they might snuff their lights out in the device seen here.

Above: Royal Warrant, Floris, Jermyn Street, SW1. Several shops in this affluent part of London bear the Royal Warrant, a much sought-after endorsement.

Left: Shop sign, County Fire Office, Piccadilly, W1.

Above: Bilingual street sign, Woodseer Street, E1.

Right: Street sculpture, Bermondsey Wall, SE16. This little girl is one of a trio of figures sculpted by Diane Gorvin as a tribute to Dr Salter who was a well-liked local councillor and MP. The other figures are Dr Salter himself and a cat. The little girl is Joyce.

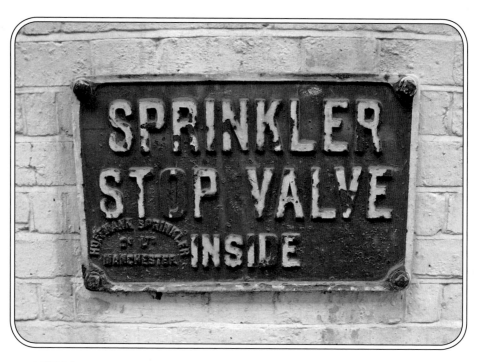

Above: Sprinkler Stop Valve, Eyre Street Hill, EC1.

Left: Standpipe, Chiswick Mall, W4. These items of street furniture are becoming rare.

Steelyard, Leonard Street, EC2. Former warehouse premises renovated as apartments but retaining evidence of their previous use with this steelyard or derrick device.

Temple Bar stands at the junction of Fleet Street and Strand and marks the boundary between the Cities of London and Westminster. Wren's Temple Bar of the 1670s was taken down in 1878 and re-erected in Hertfordshire. It has returned to the City and now stands looking somewhat self-conscious in St Paul's Churchyard. It was replaced by this king-size piece of street furniture designed by Horace Jones.

Above: Surviving tram tracks at the entrance to the former Kingsway Tram Subway, WC2. The last trams ran in 1952. Trams and their tracks were once such familiar features of urban London's streets.

Right: Wine Office Court is the narrow and rather gloomy passage leading to the 'Cheese'. Some idea of the historic nature of the place is provided for those who want to know.

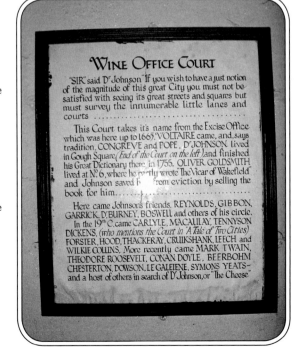

WINE OFFICE COURT

"SIR" said Dr Johnson "If you wish to have a just notion of the magnitude of this great City you must not be satisfied with seeing its great streets and squares but must survey the innumerable little lanes and courts . . . .

This Court takes it's name from the Excise Office which was here up to 1665. VOLTAIRE came, and, says tradition, CONGREVE and POPE, Dr JOHNSON lived in Gough Square (*End of the Court on the left*) and finished his Great Dictionary there in 1755. OLIVER GOLDSMITH lived at No 6, where he partly wrote The Vicar of Wakefield" and Johnson saved h... from eviction by selling the book for him. . . . .

Here came Johnson's friends, REYNOLDS, GIBBON, GARRICK, Dr BURNEY, BOSWELL and others of his circle. In the 19th C. came CARLYLE, MACAULAY, TENNYSON DICKENS, (*who mentions the Court in 'A Tale of Two Cities*) FORSTER, HOOD, THACKERAY, CRUIKSHANK, LEECH and WILKIE COLLINS. More recently came MARK TWAIN, THEODORE ROOSEVELT, CONAN DOYLE, BEERBOHM CHESTERTON, DOWSON, LE GALEIENE, SYMONS YEATS— and a host of others in search of Dr Johnson, or "The Cheese"

Lamp guiding the way to Ye Olde Cheshire Cheese, Wine Office Court, EC4.